LAW
AS LOGIC AND
EXPERIENCE

BY

MAX RADIN

THE LAWBOOK EXCHANGE, LTD.
Clark, New Jersey

ISBN 9781584770084 (hardcover)
ISBN 9781616192709 (paperback)

Lawbook Exchange edition 2000, 2012

The quality of this reprint is equivalent to the quality of the original work.

THE LAWBOOK EXCHANGE, LTD.

33 Terminal Avenue
Clark, New Jersey 07066-1321

*Please see our website for a selection of our other publications
and fine facsimile reprints of classic works of legal history:*
www.lawbookexchange.com

Library of Congress Cataloging-in-Publication Data

Radin, Max, 1880-1950.
    Law as logic and experience / by Max Radin.
        p. cm.
Originally published: New Haven : Yale UniversityPress, 1940.
Includes bibliographical references and index.
ISBN 1-58477-008-2 (cl. : alk. paper)
1. Law — Methodology. 2. Logic. 3. Experience. I. Title.
K213.R33 1999
340'. 1—dc21   99-30670
                                                         CIP

Printed in the United States of America on acid-free paper

LAW
AS LOGIC AND
EXPERIENCE

BY

MAX RADIN

NEW HAVEN
YALE UNIVERSITY PRESS
LONDON   HUMPHREY MILFORD · OXFORD UNIVERSITY PRESS
1940

PREFACE

This book in the main is made up of the lectures delivered in April, 1940, at the Yale Law School on the Storrs Foundation. For the opportunity of delivering them as part of so notable a series, I am deeply grateful to the faculty of the Law School. If the lecture tone is some what too apparent, I can only ask the indulgence of my readers.

The examination of law that is here attempted in no sense intends to strike a middle course between "conceptualism" and "realism." Lawyers in practice are likely to be realists in what they do and conceptualists in what they say. The appellate judges whose written opinions loom so large in legal discourse seem equally to be split personalities, frequently realistic enough in the results they seek to attain and rigidly conceptualistic in the reasons they assign for seeking to attain them.

If "conceptualism" were recognized for what it is, an inescapable form of the language of the law, it could do little harm. It could be taken to be a form of procedure, mischievous only when the concepts are made ends in themselves, or given an objective existence. The concepts—that is to say, the general terms which lawyers use for the sake of ready communication with each other—may then be arranged in logical and mathematical relations for the eminently practical purpose of further facilitating that communication—in all of which it is essential to abide by the fine economy of William of Occam who knew that

concepts were names, and not things, and who had so
short a way of dealing with them.

But if Occam's *entia non sunt multiplicanda prae-
ter necessitatem* is the guiding principle of legal realists, who ought to take no umbrage at being called
nominalists, they may not supplement it with a
haughty insistence on Newton's *hypotheses non fingo.*
They cannot help constructing hypotheses because
they cannot reach experience except by such imagined constructions, and experience is what they are
after.

That is the burden of this book. And it further attempts to reaffirm an ancient doctrine, that economy
of effort, precision of phrase, engrossed interest in
human experience are not of themselves enough, even
if present in a superlative degree. It would be arro-
gant for lawyers to assume the task of establishing
justice in the world, if by justice we mean a perfect
state of society. But if the law dare not hope to end
in justice so understood, it may—indeed, it must—
begin with another kind of justice, with justice as a
sense of humanity. To omit it is to offend against
both realism and conceptualism, since humanity is the
stuff with which lawyers busy themselves and since
any formula of legal discourse inconsistent with the
hypothesis that men are interested in each other's
welfare is, or should be, bad law.

The law has been called a grave study. It is undoubtedly a difficult and an exacting one. Nonetheless there are those who take delight in it. But the delight that lawyers take in their craft can never quite
be the pleasure that mathematicians find in the complexities of pure mathematics. There is no such thing

as "pure" law. The profession of the law in all its forms has never detached itself completely from the various kinds of human activity out of which it grew. It is essential that no complete detachment ever takes place.

MAX RADIN.

Berkeley, California.

Lawyer. What makes you say, that the study of the law is less rational than the study of the mathematics?

Philosopher. I say not that; for all study is rational, or nothing worth: but I say, that the great masters of the *mathematics* do not so often err as the great professors of the law.

THOMAS HOBBES: A Dialogue between a Philosopher & a Student of the Common Laws of England.

LAW AS LOGIC AND EXPERIENCE

I.

T HE great man whose most famous legal utterance will serve as text for the following pages was a lawyer, a scholar, and a thinker, but his impress on his time is primarily that of a lofty and highly individualized personality. All classes of men were conscious of him. While he lived, it was never possible for those who hated democracy and feared liberty to be altogether at their ease. He became, in the minds of powerful and rapacious persons, the lingering doubt whether their rapacity was quite powerful enough, and we know that largely because of Oliver Wendell Holmes it often turned out not to be, to the greater glory of our American heritage.

Now, what he accomplished illustrates his doctrine. It was not the irresistible force of his syllogisms that gave him his position and authority, nor yet his felicitous and subtle style. It was the accumulated tradition of the highest range of intellectual experience that the country could muster, an experience that seemed embodied in him, so that his words and ideas were charged with the life that America has lived when it was lived best. Certainly to the very measurable extent that he helped to make American law, it was human experience and not abstract logic that quickened the mass.

When Holmes said that the life of the law was experience and not logic,[1] he was, as he knew, in opposi-

1. *The Common Law* (Boston, 1881), p. 1. "The life of the law has not been logic: it has been experience."

tion to an idea about law which was of respectable but not immeasurable antiquity. The Stoic Chrysippus in the third century B.C. had defined law as right reason proceeding from supreme Zeus, commanding what should be done and forbidding what should not be done.[2] This definition, filtered through Cicero, the Renaissance, and Coke, was restated with unessential modifications by Blackstone[3] and thus came to determine the attitude toward law on the part of judges and lawyers in Wichita, Kansas, and Grass Valley, California—a far cry, we may concede, from Soli in Cilicia, where Chrysippus was born.

It is curious that the very words of Holmes are contradicted in advance by the form which this idea takes in a famous formula of the man who was called the "oracle of the common law." "Reason," said Sir Edward Coke, "is the life of the law."[4] The issue seems to be joined sharply enough between experience and reason, which is, of course, logic.

The Stoic definition has the merit of being one of the most complete instances of pleonasm that we can imagine. For, if law is right, it could proceed from nowhere else than from the mind of the Stoic Zeus and it could not help commanding what ought to be done and forbidding the opposite. And if we take

2. von Arnim, H., *Fragmenta Stoicorum Vet.*, II, 295; III, 201. It is the favorite definition of Cicero. Cf. *De Legibus*, I, 618; II, 8.

3. *Commentaries on the Laws of England*, I, 44, §43. "Municipal law, thus understood, is properly defined to be 'a rule of civil conduct, prescribed by the supreme power in a state, commanding what is right and forbidding what is wrong.'" Cf. *ibid.*, pp. 53–54. Chitty in his note *ad loc.* goes back to the exact words of Chrysippus. The phrase of Blackstone is quoted often enough in cases. Cf. *Budd* vs. *State*, 22 Tenn. 483, 490.

4. 1 *Institutes*, 138.

what is left of the definition when we omit the reference to Zeus and to forbidding and commanding, even the words "right reason" themselves, the *orthos logos*, turn out to be a pleonasm, since there could be no crooked reason and the Latin translation of *orthos*, which is *rectus*, became a noun that gave us both the English word for "rights" and the Continental word for "law." "Reason," again, is only another example of this rightness. Reason was always right, and right always reason.

But whether the famous definition of Chrysippus is to be condensed into a single word, or kept as two, it seems to be as removed from human experience as anything can well be. Not for nothing is "right"— *orthos, recta*—a term of geometry, and "reason"— *logos, ratio*—a term of arithmetic, or better, a term of accounting. The formula established the notion that law is a kind of mathematics which might be handled by clerks who need never be asked at all to endure the painful operation of living; and this notion has always been singularly bewitching because it promises us the easy achievement of the great goals of judicial administration, certainty, impartiality, and permanence.

A system of mathematics needs a notation, and systems of law have attempted to provide this in the form of technical terms which have earned for lawyers much of the animosity with which they are regarded by laymen. We cannot have our right reason without some fairly close attention to words and to verbal discriminations, any more than mathematics can get along for any but the greatest minds without taking considerable pains over notation. The power-

ful and effective notation for the integral calculus
which was devised by Leibnitz was adopted readily in
France and very slowly in England; it was this fact
which helped to give to eighteenth-century France its
marked leadership in science and mathematics, and
played a part in inspiring that confidence in rational-
izing processes which made the French Revolution
appear not as a cataclysmic upheaval but merely as
an obviously fair and feasible plan of reorganization
—one which would doubtless seem today to meet the
requirements of the Chandler Act or the defunct Section 77B.

Certainly words and terms are not contemptible in
law. In law as logic they are the elements that are
added, subtracted, divided, differentiated, and inte-
grated; and if they are inexact or ambiguous we
shall have the kind of equations we deserve. In law as
experience the terms we use are surely of more than
minor importance. It is well enough to say that we
are concerned with ideas and not with words, or, going back to Hindustan or at any rate to Mr. Samuel
Johnson's dictionary, that words are the daughters of
earth and things are the sons of heaven.[5] Law, I fear,
finds difficulties of jurisdiction, let us say, and of
domicile, when it tries to deal with the sons of heaven,
and feels more at home with the daughters of earth—
at least most of us should, if we were the law.

Whether we like it or not, law as experience, as
well as law as logic, is bound to be a matter of words
to a very considerable degree. We cannot have legal
experience without communication and we cannot

5. Johnson used the phrase in the Preface to his dictionary. It is
quoted by Sir William Jones as a Hindustani proverb.

communicate with each other in dumb show. And if we use words, we had better be careful of them, since the minutest changes carry tremendous implications. We have only to think of the word "law" itself, unarticled, unadjectived, unqualified, a vast body without limits of space and time, and to realize that the mere addition of the definite article contracts it at once in space if not in time. It ceases to be a legal philosophy or a universal policy and becomes the mere "municipal" law of the seventeenth and eighteenth centuries, a thing cramped into the confines of a single state. And by doing nothing more than changing the definite article to the indefinite one, by speaking of "a law" instead of "the law" or "law," we descend into the piffling particularity of an ephemeral statute. If we can do all this with the most contemptible of parts of speech, the lowly article, what may we not expect from the fullest utilization of all the resources of style and diction?

Again, the fact that in English "law" and "right" are two different words has saved us the mass of dialectical involutions by which, principally in Germany but also in Italy and France, men have spun out libraries in order to set forth the difference between subjective and objective law, nearly all of which— except the part that has an even more baleful source —is the progeny of a mere verbal ambiguity; to wit, the fact that in German, Italian, French, and Spanish "law" and "right" are the same word: *Recht, droit, diritto, derecho*. The more baleful source to which I refer is the romantic and pretentious metaphysics of nineteenth-century Germany. There could be no better example of the dangers inherent in the clouds of glory or of any less resplendent vapor which words inevitably trail after them. We cannot help the fact that they do, but we ought, I think, not to assist the cloud-gathering any more than we are compelled to by the fact that we must use words for every kind of legal expression.

For the logic of the law, we should like a mathematical notation instead of words. We may recall that Cardozo sighed for a logarithm.[6] The operations of mathematics have always been held up to us as the ultimate goal of all science. They have a compelling logic and result in an unshakable certainty. How different from the halting and qualified guesses of the social sciences! And above all, how different from the law which even among the social sciences sits far below the salt!

The mathematically minded, however, are prone to forget that to the uninitiated in modern mathematical research the pure and irrefragable logic of mathematics is illustrated only by such introductory disciplines as algebra and geometry—Euclidean geometry, incidentally. Now, in mathematics of this stage— I say nothing of the fearsome developments of recent years—we should be no better off, so far as the law is concerned, than if we held to Chrysippus. If the Stoic formula was a pleonasm, algebra and geometry are an immense and protracted tautology. The thirteen books into which our extant manuscripts of Euclid's *Elements* are divided are manifold and patient repetitions of the statements at the beginning of Book I, the "definitions," "postulates," and "common no-

6. Cardozo, Benjamin, *The Paradoxes of Legal Science* (1927), p. 1.

tions." However involved and intricate the final theorems sound, they cannot possibly add an idea—not the smallest—that was not originally expressed in the definitions. Similarly, algebra is an extremely ingenious series of variations on the theme that A equals A. If the movement in ever so right a line from the mind of Zeus is an illusion, considered as movement, legal progress by means of mathematics is equally an illusion. We cannot by logarithms and diagrams move an infinitesimal fraction of an inch ahead of the starting post.

Yet we should be other than human if we failed to cherish our illusions and particularly the illusion that our thinking can be most effectively expressed by logic or mathematics. Man is by nature an irrational creature that yearns to be rational. Since mathematics can do us little good in law for the practical purposes that we dare not disavow, we cling to it as an emotional discharge. We can think out mathematical metaphors which will relieve us from being too oppressively conscious of experience.

Mr. Lasswell has habituated his hearers and readers to the phrase, "frames of reference."[7] I should be quite content to adopt the expression because of its mathematical suggestions, as my favorite mathematical metaphor for the double orientation of law, if it were not for the fact that it is not really a frame that I have in mind but something simpler. We shall do better, perhaps, if we have recourse to that admirable device of Descartes, the two ordinates—or the ordinate and abscissa—one line running in one direction

7. Lasswell, Harold, *Psychopathology and Politics* (1931); *World Politics and Personal Insecurity* (1935).

and the other intersecting it, generally at right angles. Any curve or figure of any sort in a plane surface may be exhaustively described by reference to these two coördinates and fixed permanently and precisely by its distances from both.

This, it seems to me, is a better metaphor to use for the two diverse ways in which the law must be stated than most others that have been canvassed. We dare not abandon human experience and we do not wish to appear illogical. An Italian mathematician declared that "experience can never give us anything logically necessary."[8] If we accepted this doctrine, we might make logic and experience eternal parallels in the law or, at least, asymptotes, lines that perpetually approached parallelism without quite achieving it. The suggestion stirs in me a faint nostalgia for the psychophysical parallelism of my boyhood manuals, that fine and easy doctrine which asserted the fundamental disparity of mind and matter, and explained their apparent reciprocal influences as an astounding and unremitting sequence of coincidences.

If one of our ordinates is human experience and the other is right reason, the *orthos logos* emanating from the mind of Zeus, we can play with the pictures presented and call attention to the fact that the farther these two lines are prolonged, the farther the points of prolongation will be from each other. But we can also call attention to the fact that experience and reason do meet, at least once, at the point of intersection, even if never again. Anyone who desires

8. Levi, Adolfo, *L'Indeterminismo nella filosofia francese contemp.* (1904), p. 3: "*L'Esperienza non può mai dare qualche cosa di logicamente necessario ed universale.*"

may continue the game further and make a complete analytical geometry of the law, for whatever purpose of exposition or entertainment he has in mind. It is no great matter and it is no great help.[9]

The process of logic, as of mathematics, is always described as something moving forward. The very word "process" implies that. That this is an illusion, has already been noted. But it is doubly illusory, if the actual application of logical methods to law is looked at closely. For the most part, as Cardozo has so brilliantly shown us, the movement can best be described as backward and not forward.[10] We have our conclusion before we have our major premise. It is as though the theorem of the square of the hypotenuse were known first, and that from this we deduced that the angles of a triangle are equal to two right angles or that the area of a rectangle is found by multiplying one side by the side perpendicular to it. Cardozo was not proclaiming a legal philosophy but noting a fact. That is to say, he noted it as a fact in the genesis of any particular syllogism or mathematical demonstration into which legal discussion is put.

Legal discourse puts on its full mathematical disguise only when misguided persons lecture on jurisprudence. Normally lawyers who talk of law have as little to do with abscissas and ordinates as they have with any other form of notation and diagram. But while they may abjure diagrams, they cannot help

9. An interesting mathematical terminology for law is suggested by Mr. Frederick C. Hicks in his *Legal Research* (2d ed., 1933), pp. 11–25. It takes into account a calculus of variations of behavior on the part of men who make the law.

10. Cardozo, Benjamin, *The Nature of the Judicial Process* (1925). Cf. especially pp. 28–47.

dealing with words, with a great many words indeed, and in some cases with words that are heaped by hundreds of thousands on each other to explain other words. By the time we are through with them we have certainly gone a long way from either human experience or from that straight line of reasoning which discriminates between what is to be done and what left undone. At every step in legal development there is always a tendency to call law back to either or both of these points of departure, to the human experience in which the law lives or to the source of its rationality. The latter, you will remember, is by Stoic doctrine, the mind of Zeus, and it is this fairly remote origin that we shall first attempt to seek.

We know that we can follow a good deal of our legal reasoning back a considerable distance. The law reaches the ordinary man through a professional person whose business the law is. These lawyers undoubtedly declare what is to be done and what is to be avoided, just what Chrysippus said it was the law's function to do. They are constantly at work in and out of courts telling specific persons that they must refrain from specific acts or must perform these acts. A corporation head is informed that a large part of the money his company has accumulated in the past year will almost surely be considered taxable income for that year by the Bureau of Internal Revenue and that the company had better appropriate money to pay it. We can readily follow this back to the Internal Revenue Act and this to the constitutional grant of taxing power to the Federal or state government. If the Constitution is not quite the mind of Zeus, it is as far as we need go. But, in other instances, we shall have to go farther, because the Constitution takes a great many things for granted. When I assert that no one may lawfully take away my property except under special conditions, this act, which I vehemently declare should not be done, is not really derived from the Constitution at all. There is a conduit, shall we say, by which we may pass through the Constitution into the less precisely charted sea in which we must seek the source of property and of due process of law.

The Stoic Zeus lived in the empyrean but we do not have to go quite so far even for property and due process of law. It is enough for us if we can find property protected and a regulatory system recognized as early as the first session of the Exchequer of the Norman king in England, and if our straight line of reason can be terminated there, that will amply satisfy us.

It will not, of course, satisfy social philosophers who will insist on making the perilous flight higher and higher. A social philosophy is sometimes forced on us against our will, and when it is, we must, I suppose, reluctantly take off for the empyrean, but we shall not have to do so just yet. What all this accumulation of figures of speech comes to, is merely the fact that the attraction which logic has for the law is not derived from an examination of the entire process —even in the sense of Chrysippus. If we choose to express this logic in a series of syllogisms in which the duty to pay a tax is the last conclusion—what is called a sorites—it is only the latter end that we have examined at all. When we got well into the middle and long before we reached the source of right reason, we were unaccountably persuaded that logic had triumphed, and we leaped lightheartedly over the gap that still separated us from a premise of premises. Lovely and satisfactory as logic is as a method, we can make it satisfactory in result only by ignoring the gap.

Bacon called attention to that.[11] Those in his day who were most intent on following the line of reason which is—I say it with diffidence—often the line of least resistance were very bitter against a law that depended upon *placita*, arbitrary assertions of will. This was a controversial word in the furious war of words that Bacon's contemporary and enemy Coke conducted against Bacon and all reorganizers or would-be reorganizers of the perfect common law. The civil law was derived, said Coke, from the *placet* of an absolute king—the "our good pleasure" of haughty monarchs. Not so the severely rational common law. But there is a *placet* at the beginning of your reasoning, retorted Bacon, which you choose to disregard. And if you look at the authority of those who issued the *placet*, you might prefer that it should be a wise and responsible monarch.

With their utmost efforts, accordingly, those who seek to make a mathematics or a logic of law cannot make it pure Euclidean. We can get a geometry out of "common notions"—that is to say, notions so apparently easy to understand that only analytic philosophers will question them, and so easy to apply that the limited range of experience of simple men can verify them. A geometry of law has to depend somewhere on a human interposition or on a divine source that speaks an extremely human language,

11. *Advancement of Learning*, III, xxi, §5.

the language of *sic volo, sic iubeo*. We shall be lucky
indeed if only one such arbitrary interpolation is
needed and that at the source. But that single one
colors all that follows since succeeding syllogisms will,
as we have seen, merely restate it.

If we then gladly abandon logic as the life of the
law and turn to experience, the first question that
must be answered is: "Whose experience?" And certainly the answer is inevitable. Not the experience of
lawyers in any of the Protean guises that lawyers or
quasi-lawyers assume, advocates, attorneys, judges,
administrators, or legislators. Nothing of that sort.
The experience in question is evidently the experience of nonlawyers, the great mass of the community
who live in separate households as members of families, who go to their daily tasks as employees or employers, who are born and marry and die and are
duly buried—death and burial are, I assure you,
hugely important experiences in the law as well as in
ordinary life.

And of this we may be assured. These persons in
whose experiences the law is alive, when they rise up
and lie down, when they go forth and return, are as
wholly unaware that they have had anything like a
legal experience as Monsieur Jourdain was that he
had been talking prose all his life. As a matter of
fact, they would have violently repudiated the suggestion, since they entertain the fervent hope—or say
they do—when they think about the law at all, that
they will have the least to do with it that is possible.
The law means to them judges, juries, sheriffs, jails,
policemen, and tax collectors; or else leases, deeds,
mortgages, wills, articles of incorporation, policies of

insurance—a mass of paper that must be signed, sealed, and delivered, in which signing, sealing, and delivering there is a deal of actual and potential jeopardy. When a nonlawyer affixes his signature to a legal document he usually does so with undisguised misgiving. Some day a hectoring attorney will thunder at him, "Is this your signature?" and on his faltering admission will turn with a look of cruel elation to a jury or judge.

If the experiences of the usual run of mankind are the life of the law, it is at least curious that the vast majority of these experiences are not recognized as such when they are undergone. A small minority of them are so recognized. In the case of this small minority, those who undergo them know that they are legal and call them by that name. The bringing of a suit at law, the making or the foreclosure of a mortgage, the signing of a lease, or the eviction of a tenant, the arrest and trial of an offender, the execution of a criminal—all these things are indubitably legal experiences. The tendency of those who think about the law—laymen and lawyers—is to confine law to these particular things, and to things somewhat like them, to speak, when they become analysts, of "acts-in-the-law" or "facts-of-the-law," *juristiche Handlungen* or *juristiche Tatsachen*.

That, I think, falsifies the picture materially. These matters are known and recognized as legal, because they have always been so labeled. The least lawyerlike of laymen knows them for what they are and is compelled for the nonce and with immense resistance to look at them as a lawyer does. If he has had considerable experience with them, his resistance and apprehension disappear and he thinks, often rightly, that in these matters he is as good a lawyer as the most fully credentialed and licensed member of the bar. Insurance and real estate brokers make no secret of their confidence in their own legal skill, a confidence which within the limited field in which they operate is quite justified. And the professional litigant, the Peter Peebles of any generation, has nothing but contempt for the lawyers whom he inveigles into representing him and whom he does not need in the least. Perhaps it will one day be proved that every person is secretly a lawyer at heart, and the fear and contempt for the law which he vociferously proclaims, as well as his animosity toward lawyers, will be shown to be merely examples of frustration. Psychologists are invited to examine this promising and neglected field of investigation.

The persons who deal habitually with acts that are like those just described, which are known to be legal acts because they are part of the devices which professional lawyers have created for their professional and technical purposes, have no difficulty, I have said, in recognizing their legal character. And other laymen who deal only occasionally with such acts equally recognize them. They are unmistakably labeled. But these acts and the group to which they belong are the only things so labeled. Altogether they constitute the body of facts we call legal procedure, in the large sense in which that term includes evidence and the preparation of documents, a vitally important body in the history of law. We shall have to recur to procedure, but for the present it is necessary only to mention the fact that the matters of procedure are not the "acts-in-the-law" that analysts have attempted to segregate and that whatever their historical origin, they are now assumed to be merely a mechanism to enable lawyers to deal with other facts.

Since procedure is mechanism, it has a great advantage. Its constituent elements were devised to achieve a specific result and nothing else and were marked with terms that would make them unambiguously recognizable. We may be in doubt whether a document is a contract. We are not likely to be in doubt about a summons. And when lawyers talked of this peculiar and special province of theirs—and they originally talked of little else and still talk more about it than of anything else—they could speak in terms that were fairly close to terms of logic and mathematics. They began with a training, therefore, that may have given them a false notion of the readiness with which facts can be forced into terminologies.

But they realized that after all, their procedure, their legal activity par excellence, was directed to the manipulation of other facts. Those other facts constitute human experience, most of human experience. Are they legal facts at all? Or are some of them legal facts and not others, as we currently assume? The ordinary person, whose experiences these facts are, does not consider them legal facts when they occur. How do they become legal facts, if they ever do?

It seems to me the answer is simple. They become legal facts just as soon as a lawyer undertakes to deal with them professionally. Talking to lawyers, I can venture to say he has the Midas touch. Whatever he handles becomes gold, since obviously law is golden. Nonlawyers will charge him with a wholly contrary alchemy, but under no circumstances can it be claimed that anything is immune from his touch. Religion and family relations, artistic merit and literary originality, the fidelity of spouses and the loyalty of friends, all these things have at one time or another become legal facts, because they have been examined by lawyers in court before other lawyers. There is, indeed, no incident of life which is withdrawn from legal examination by its character or essential nature, and about which some indubitably legal pronouncement could not be made, if the occasion arose.

The experience which is the life of the law is, therefore, not the experience of lawyers but of nonlawyers and has of itself no legal content or coloring or function. If this experience is to be considered—and I think it is—as the subject matter of the law, it must be because the law has no subject matter of its own, with the indicated exception of procedure. Just as W. K. Clifford defined matter as nonmatter in motion, so legal experience seems to be nonlegal experience set in motion by lawyers. And since it remains nonlegal even when lawyers handle it, as it was before they meddled with it and will be nonlegal after they are through with it, it is well to note that this legal motion or coloring, given to the stream of experience by lawyers, is local and ephemeral. Only occasionally does the glint of gold which we Midases give to it appear at all—as a matter of fact, only while we are actually touching it. As soon as we remove our hands, it is seen to have the ordinary color of everyday life, which is perhaps even better than gold.

You remember Chrysippus and his progeny—especially through Sir William Blackstone—and how

they all spoke of the law as something that told us
what to do and what to leave undone. That, one might
imagine, is a large order. To do what we ought to do
and leave undone what we ought not to do is nearly
the whole duty of man. If law does all this, what is the
function of ethics, of religion, of morals, of education? If law is an "ought" science, so are they. Does
it mean that we divide the P's and Q's we are to mind,
and turn some of them—the P's let us say—over to
ethics and religion, and keep the Q's? Sometimes that
is almost feasible, but only very rarely. In the vast
majority of cases, it is the same "ought" that is insisted upon by all these depositaries of the categorical
imperative, and an "ought" in relation to the same
actions. To knock a man down in a busy thorough-
fare is, it has been remarked, at one and the same
time illegal, immoral, irreligious, unmannerly, and an
interference with traffic. Evidently if law meddles
with human experience with the intention of directing
it, as ethics and religion certainly do, it cannot assume exclusive jurisdiction.

There is one further matter to note. If it were
true that the task of determining what ought to be
done and what left undone were really the law's, large
as this sphere is, it would fall quite short of what law
in practice does deal with, and what for most communities it was at first intended primarily to be concerned with. Not only what we ought to do or not to
do, but what we may do if we choose or leave undone
if we prefer, is the business of the law. This notion
of liberty, both in the medieval and the modern sense,
is not an incidental or exceptional element in the law.
It covers the larger group of the situations in which

we contemplate the law at all. Hohfeld spoke of these situations as involving privileges[12] and whether the word was well chosen or not, he found most of his fellow jurisprudents persistently refusing to understand what he meant. A privilege in Hohfeld's use of the word was not a special and exceptional sort of right. It was merely the negation of someone else's right, or one's own duty. In nearly every law suit, judgment for the defendant is a judgment that the defendant had a privilege.

That this relation is at least as important as the relation of "ought" or "ought not" was not a discovery of Hohfeld but was just as vigorously asserted by Hobbes who used it in a criticism of a characteristically wrongheaded doctrine of Coke.[13] "Law obligeth me," he says in his *Dialogue of the Common Laws*, "to do or forbear the doing of something: and therefore it layeth upon me an obligation. But my right is a liberty left me by the law to do anything which the law forbids me not, and to leave undone anything which the law commands me not. Did Sir Edward Coke see no difference between being bound and being free?" It is not surprising that lawyers have repeated Coke's violence and have ignored Hobbes, although, when they are engaged in their business and not reverently repeating the pronouncement of their oracles, lawyers are fully aware that the relation of "ought" and "ought not"—the duty-right relation—is somewhat less important than the relation expressed by "may"—the "liberty," for which a good word no longer exists in English, since "license" has become a bad word.

That is to say, a description of law, which derives from the notion that law "regulates" our conduct, errs not only by excess but almost equally by defect. For purposes of legal discourse, the part of human experience which the law declines to direct, or to attempt to direct, is nonetheless very much its affair. The life of the law includes as one of its notable elements the sense of being free from legal direction.

It is one of the instances which antirationalists—I do not class Holmes in this group at all—are likely to disregard. We may, if we like, think of a logical process as consisting exclusively in the rearrangement that a mind imposes on life but there are examples of very close coincidence, moments at which the ordinate of logic does intersect the abscissa of experience. The logical contradictory of a duty to act is not a duty to refrain, as seems to be implied in so much legal discussion—and not wholly abstract legal discussion—but it is the absence of any duty. And in actual experience, what is felt under such circumstances is just precisely that. The absence of a duty is something that can actually be felt by human beings and is consequently very much a matter of experience. Hohfeld worked out the relationship between his privilege and its contradictories—which he mistakenly termed opposites—and its converses—which he mistakenly called correlatives. His errors in terminology did not affect the correctness of his

mathematical analysis.[14] What is interesting is that
the result of his mathematics was to bring into promi-
nence a relationship of which the negative side—ordinarily a pure abstraction, because it is a minus quantity—coincides in human experience with a thoroughly real feeling, the sense of being free from
compulsion.

Experience, so far as it consists of conduct of men
toward other men, can thus be placed in categories
which will involve something more than "ought" and
"ought not," something which will include a contradictory of "ought" for which there is no unequivocal
English phrase, although "may" is an approximation. And the vastly greater part of this experience
is eminently nonlegal. The law makes forays into it
from time to time, but does not keep its booty long.
Certainly in their myriad upon myriad of daily acts,
men are not conscious of being directed by the kind of
law that is the business of professional lawyers and
would resent such direction.

Are they directed by other systems of obligatory
rules—also necessarily involving "ought" and "may,"
systems which are classed as ethics and religion, or
those which are classed as manners and fashion? I
think it may be said here, as in the case of law, that
there is in most cases no conscious submission to this
direction just as there is no rejection of it. Conduct,
which is expressed by refraining from action quite as
well as by action, is not a thing we can decline to do.
And evidently we do not take thought about rights

14. Cf. "A Restatement of Hohfeld," 51 *Harvard Law Review*,
1141–1164.

and duties before we act or refrain. It is a matter of instincts, and, even more often, of habits which are the result of impulses almost or quite unconscious. Our conduct is less a series of disparate acts than a continuous process of social living, a stream of activity. It follows a routine, and it is cut into segments only when we think or talk about it.

This routine, we know, is not quite uniform. There are waves and cycles in social conduct as well as in business affairs. There have been periods of strictness and looseness in adult sex relations in Western society, periods in which divorce was rare and those in which it was frequent, periods in which family solidarity was strong and others in which it was weak. It is unlikely that the beginning of each cyclical change was produced by the conscious and voluntary determination to observe any type of norm—religious, ethical, or legal—or to refuse to observe them. It is, on the other hand, quite likely that many of these norms—especially legal ones—are subsequent rationalizations of any of these larger shifts of social conduct. And these rationalizations are quite as capable of showing cyclical ebbs and floods as the conduct which they formulate. Divorce and family obligations are matters which lawyers not infrequently deal with and which are consequently often made legal matters, but no one will seriously contend that lax divorce laws have created the relative readiness of modern Americans to dissolve marriages. The sequence is clearly the reverse of this. An increased readiness to dissolve marriages has produced lax divorce laws.

That is not to say that social conduct is never determined by norms, in the sense of rules externally set and consciously regarded as authoritative. To deny that the Church prohibition of divorce during the Middle Ages made many marriages permanent which today would be dissolved, would be to reject obvious facts. The same could be said for a sense of filial respect in communities in which both tradition and authoritative religion make such respect a duty of highest obligation. Adult sons have obeyed their fathers in communities where such a duty was formally inculcated by law or expressly asserted, under circumstances under which obedience would be refused today.

Even purely legal norms may be factors in determining conduct in this field of family relations. The rule that the half-blood did not inherit and the rule of primogeniture had far greater force and wider application in England than elsewhere. These rules did not arise out of a weakened fraternal bond, since English feudal society was not notably different from that of the Continent. On the Continent these two rules yielded to influences which were less successful in England, where they were extended so that they became general principles of the land law. Their obvious effect in England was appreciably to relax the fraternal bond in that country, at any rate in those social groups in which the rules had significance, the upper class of landed proprietors. It is one of the rare instances in which a legal norm can be credited with a real effect on family conduct and on the pattern of family life.

Again, in the wholly different field of business experience, the patterns and classifications have obviously not been created under the direction of lawyers.

In Europe there was the historical reason that merchants had their own law and their own courts for centuries, and that in these courts a differentiated class of exclusively mercantile lawyers did not grow up. When mercantile custom began to be handled by lawyers, it was pretty well fixed and as it changed and transformed itself to suit new conditions produced by modern economic revolutions it asked little help of the lawyers.

Mercantile custom, it is true, was not always an unconscious growth, not always composed of merely accidental ways of acting, inadvertently imitated by others who noticed them. On the contrary, these customs were not infrequently set rules deliberately worked out and written down, issued to large groups by persons who claimed authority to issue them and were granted this authority. But these groups were not lawyers—merely old or experienced or skillful or successful members of the groups themselves.

Even when lawyers undertook specifically to interfere in mercantile custom they were often only slightly heeded. The common law denied that a partnership was an entity and strained itself to deal with partnership problems as though it were not. That is to say, it refused to accept the convenient shorthand of calling it one. Merchants, on the contrary, had always done so and thereby immensely facilitated their discourse as well as their systems of accounting. Recently, of course, lawyers have been compelled to speak of partnerships as businessmen do, and have done so with obvious and slightly ill-tempered reluctance. But businessmen have successfully ignored the efforts of lawyers to make them use legal language about what they understood better than the lawyers did.

Most of human experience is accordingly habitual and unconscious and consequently only very rarely determined by conscious application of norms, least of all legal norms. And when norms are used, they are based on standards which were created either by systems of regulation like ethics or religion, or by set quasi-legislative determinations within the groups themselves.

What is the function of lawyers in all this? If experience is the life of the law, how does the law live on it, if men manage their conscious and unconscious experience with so little reference to the law? Well, there is one method of approach which will seem to laymen highly characteristic. Lawyers may not succeed in changing or directing human experience, but they find it necessary to talk about it and to talk a great deal about it.

When we thought of law as logic we found we were dealing with words. To be sure, since logic is mathematics, we were looking for a notation in which our terms should be precise and unequivocal so that they could be put into equations and produce calculable— that is, rational—results. No such words are available, although the effort to use words in that way in logic is a continuing approximation. But when lawyers talk of human experience, they must completely forego attempts to use logical formulas.

Experience cannot really be described in words at all. Words can only suggest and point at experience and make that experience intelligible by using some striking element as a sign or symbol. I hesitate to use the word "symbol" because an eminent Yale professor has in a way preëmpted that word for legal discussion, but I am thinking of the symbolic character of language not quite as Thurman Arnold uses the term, as an emotionally charged cryptogram through which for good or ill results that are not avowed can be achieved. I mean symbol as part of the problem of meaning. The word "valuation" is a term that expresses a definable act, but modern lawyers will at once have suggested to them a vast controversial literature in periodicals, and two diametrically opposed legal and social philosophies in prevailing and dissenting opinions of the Supreme Court. The picture of Mr. Justice Brandeis will flash across their minds and that of the late Mr. Justice Butler.[15] Railroads and business depressions will be on the fringes of their thought or well toward the consciously envisaged core of the picture. Valuation is a part of complex economic experience and when law deals with experience it must use the word with all the incidents that belong to the experience it suggests or symbolizes.

If we insist on the formula that things or acts are better—much better—than words, we shall be compelled to declare that discourse about experience is a poor substitute for it. But there is a great deal of cant about that formula, in spite of its ancient origin and its frequent repetition. What those who use it forget is that the formula is itself expressed in words. The part of experience we are interested in,

15. Bonbright, J. C., *The Valuation of Property* (2 vols., 1937); Commons, J. R., *Value in Law and Economics,* 2 "Law: A Century of Progress," pp. 332–345.

the actions and reactions of human beings to each
other, is not a silent film reeled off before our eyes.
Language and discourse form a very large part of it.
More than that, we cannot deal with experience at all
except when we talk about it. It is the only way in
which experience becomes a fact of human life and
not a panorama unfolded to some imagined nonhu-
man observer.

The human experience that lawyers talk about is
large enough. As has been said, nothing that can happen to a man and nothing that he can do is by its
nature withdrawn from legal examination. And the
terms lawyers use are large enough in all conscience.
The family, the home, commerce, public welfare, fac-
tory, corporation—all these words occur frequently
in legal discourse. All these words are general words,
class words, but the induction out of which the classification was made and the classification itself were not
the work of lawyers, and when lawyers use them they
take over a fixed model for these things which they
get by being members of the community, not by belonging to a limited technical profession.

The contact lawyers have with experience seems
still to elude us. When a man cautiously crosses a
street through which streams of traffic run in both
directions, he exercises care not because the law bids
him to, but because he wishes to save his neck, or at
any rate his bones, from being crushed by a heavy
and rapidly moving machine. But in the all-too-com-
mon but still exceptional contingency that he fails,
his act will be legally examined in order to find out
whether he used an exceptionally small degree of
care. Millions of people rent their homes. The law

has to do with the relatively rare case in which there is a quarrel between the landlord and the tenant about some of the relations involved in the lease. They will be unusual and exceptional relations, because if they are common and usual the law would probably never have occasion to speak of the situation at all.

It is, therefore, not the common and usual situation but the marginal and exceptional one with which the law deals. Nor is it the law that has made it marginal by establishing a general and usual class which does not obviously include the exceptional one. The general character of the class has been made by social custom, by people acting habitually in a certain way and acting in that way for reasons that have nothing to do with the law. When a marginal experience takes place, it is recognized as such by those who share it. If it were one of the common collisions of interest, the attitude that people adopt toward each other would be part of the experience itself. No one thinks that he may cross a city street without looking to the right or left. No one insists as a matter of right that he may rent an apartment, live in it, and not pay for it. The judgment of "ought" or "may" is rendered without recourse to a judge. But when the situation is one that is outside the obviously general classification, when it can be called marginal or exceptional, the law is likely enough to be asked to judge it. And in this margin of life, it speaks with authority. It sets up its own rules of "ought" and "may" which occasionally contradict those of ordinary society.

When the law speaks in these marginal situations, it uses the large language of a much more generalized experience. A man may legally disregard a gratuitous promise. This is a rather general statement. Many men and women who have never heard of the doctrine of "consideration" would take for granted that if they change their minds in a gratuitous promise, they cannot be forced by anything but a sense of propriety to carry it out. But the law's interest begins when the situation involved is a rather special one. No attempt in all likelihood will be made to enforce the promise except when it is not quite clear whether it was gratuitous or not. Suppose, for example, a benevolent employer promises the widow of a faithful employee a pension. On the faith of that she omits to seek employment for herself. May he refuse to pay? The law will say "Yes" or "No" on its own authority, although lay judgment would answer "No" almost unqualifiedly. The duty not to injure another negligently or wilfully is one created by habits of living together within relatively close quarters. The occasions for such injury are many and in general the law need not trouble itself about asserting the existence of the duty. But, in exceptional cases, it will be asked to assert or deny a duty and its answer will be derived from its own technical norms, not from any assumed answer that the public at large would give. A passer-by makes no effort to save a person struggling in the water, although he could have done it without danger to himself. It is concededly an unusual and exceptional case. The majority of common lawyers would say he might legally omit this act of mercy. The majority of nonlawyers would be of a different opinion.

That lawyers who live and work in this margin of

human experience use words which profess to cover broad areas of it and not merely the margin, is not their fault. The layman expects it of a lawyer and resents it when he is told that only a limited and narrow edge of the area is being considered. But lawyers share, of course, the inclination to make their statements as large and magnificent as possible. Most of the rules and principles of the law have been announced on occasions when all that the law actually did was to resurvey a boundary line.

In the natural sciences, an investigation of margins is often by way of an *experimentum crucis*, a means of determining the nature of a force or a substance. Bacon, who invented the term (*instantia crucis*), thought of it as a means of discovering which of two ambiguous indications is to be preferred.[16] In economics, on the other hand, I seem to remember terms like "marginal utility," "marginal price," even the "marginal farmer." The lawyer may be said, in the field of experience in which he operates, to be getting very close to the marginal utility of the generalizations which he finds ready-made and which are given to him by other social disciplines. If a "marginal" farmer is one whose existence as a farmer is quite precarious, a lawyer may be a "marginal" economist or a "marginal" sociologist. At any moment he may cease to be either and be compelled to be merely a lawyer, required to declare his judgment

16. *Novum Organum*, II, xxxvi. In the English translation they are called "Instances of the Fingerpost." Bacon goes on to say: "These I also call decisive and judicial." The phrase *experimentum crucis* seems first to have been used by Newton, *Lights and Colours*, i.

of "ought" or "may" on his own standard of valuation.

However limited the direct contact of a lawyer is with experience, he can do nothing more or less than state it in his own language. And when he does so, he will once more tend to use terms that strive for a precision words cannot completely attain. The language he uses has been developed from his contact with his own private and peculiar sphere of procedure where the approximation to precision is fairly close. It is in this language that he will attempt to state and perhaps to overstate the experience he has been asked to judge. But his statement will not after all be a falsification, and it will be less and less of one if he realizes its inadequacy.

When Elizabeth assumed her royal style, she added an et cetera to her titles. She meant to remind her people that she had not assumed all she might have done and might yet do. Above all, she might yet assume the controversial style of "Head of the Church." Any legal statement of lawyers about experience should—to use Maitland's expression—be etceterated.[17] Precision is an excellent thing, even if it cannot exhaust experience. It may well be asked of us that we be as precise as we can but we should not be asked to foreclose future contingencies. We should, therefore, warn the public and ourselves that we reserve the right to make additions. And we do not necessarily undertake to be bound by the rule of *ejusdem generis*.

Law as logic and as experience is a matter of dis-

17. Maitland, Fr., "Elizabethan Gleanings," *English Historical Review* (1900); 3 Collected Papers 157–161.

course, since the principal business of lawyers is to explain to each other what they have been doing. As logic, law attempts an approximation to mathematics and is hampered by a notation in which almost no term has a fixed and precise denotation, but it heroically struggles on to attach syllogism to syllogism, equation to equation. Often enough it is aware that it is moving backward from conclusion to major premise. And occasionally it is aware that it is not moving at all. It is most ineffective when it attempts to leap over the gaps that separate its last verifiable premise —usually a historical fact for which documentary evidence is available—to something far off in space and time, something that can be fantasied as the mind of Zeus resting eternally in the empyrean.

But this discourse, in which law as logic expresses itself, is discourse about human experience which thus becomes a part of the law when lawyers talk about it. That human experience is not wholly or mainly logical in its process is now a commonplace. It could be shown to be illogical by the mere fact that it does go somewhere, whether forward or backward or in curves or zigzags. But most certainly it does not stand still. Human experience, however, is also experience of the mind. It involves communication between persons and reactions of one person toward other persons and within the world of this moving experience the law as logic is not so wholly a deportable alien as it is sometimes declared to be by antirationalist witch hunters. We can dispense with it, but there is no reason why we should want to, just as there is no reason why we should pretend that by logic we create or change the facts we talk about.

The law as experience is desperately aware of its logical insufficiencies and the law as logic is uneasily conscious that its authority to represent experience to the mind has never been ratified. We must take these situations as we find them.

II.

WE have almost got to the point where we can see innocent, or at any rate unsuspecting, human experience turned into legal experience by getting itself publicly talked about by lawyers in their own special and peculiar and semi-mathematical language. What we must now note is that lawyers generally know pretty well what they mean although the words they use would not always indicate it.

First of all, one would not easily discover from their words that lawyers are really concerned only with human beings. They speak of the law of things, of the law of real property, of the law of oil and gas and automobiles. But they do not mean it. Nor are lawyers concerned with imaginary persons, fictitious persons, entities, juristic persons, *personnes morales*, whether these entities are called states or corporations or "society."[1] What the law busies itself with is human beings, nothing but human beings, and all human beings.

Again, the law is concerned with entire human beings, not with aspects of them or modalities or capacities. The *caput* of the Roman law, the *persona* of medieval law,[2] are words that do no harm if we know what they mean, but are pernicious in the extreme if

1. Cf. "The Endless Problem of Corporate Personality," 32 *Columbia Law Review*, 643–667.
2. Cf. *L. Schnorr vs. Carolsfeld; Geschichte der Juristischen Person,* I (1933); Hallis, Frederick, *Corporate Personality* (1930), reviewed in 31 *Columbia Law Review*, 517–519.

we do not. The notion still so widely prevalent that
the law sees only artificial constructions before it, one
man *qua* citizen, another *qua* father, subjects of
rights and duties, existing for the law only by virtue
of these rights and duties, this notion is, I think,
quite false. Human beings, for the purposes of the
law, are no more bundles of legal capacities than they
are that for the physician. They are in both connec-
tions flesh-and-blood creatures, vertebrate mammalia.
There is a story in one of Victor Hugo's novels of a
man who had let a gun carriage loose on a ship and
then saved the passengers at the risk of his life. He
was ordered to be honored as a hero and to be shot for
his misconduct. But it is to be noted that when he was
shot the hero was quite as dead as the delinquent
sailor. You cannot shoot an aspect of a man nor can
you try an aspect or give judgment for or against it.

Men—complete men—are the theme of the law.
They should, of course, be according to Sir William
Jones's verses,

> Men who their duties know,
> But know their rights and knowing, dare maintain.[3]

But they may just as well be poor and cowardly
wretches cadging for their breakfast or cringing before Führers. The law will not repudiate them so long
as they have the external and internal organs of men
or most of these organs. Unless we remember that
whatever is said in law is said about men, even if the
words used are about things and entities, we shall obviously never get to experience. The indivisible atoms

3. Ode in Imitation of Alcaeus: "What Constitutes a State?"

of the law are individual human beings. And I trust
no cyclotron will ever be devised to split them or de-
compose them.

But, if it is a whole human being that is the concern of the law, it is not an isolated human being. He
must come into relation with someone else before the
law can take notice of him. All the marginal experience in which the law lives, as well as the larger fields
of experience it enviously descries from a distance, is
social experience. What goes on within a man's mind
or body if it in no way affects the feelings or conduct
of others, if it elicits no response or reaction in any
other man, woman, or child, is legally irrelevant, however important it may be in religion, ethics, physiol-
ogy, or psychology. Equally irrelevant are the most
striking and important of terrestrial and celestial
phenomena, land and sea and air, tornadoes and hur-
ricanes, the revolutions of the planets, the precession
of the equinoxes, the emanation of the cosmic rays,
the splitting of an atom of hydrogen. Only if one
man's relation to another can plausibly—logic rears
its ugly mathematical head—be made out to depend
on any one of these things or on beliefs about them,
will the law examine these disturbances of the cosmos.
Even in that event it will examine not so much the
things or events themselves as whether it is true that a
human relation is thus dependent.

The process of making human relations part of the
experience of the law is carried on, I have said, by the
activity of lawyers who deal with these relations. How
they deal with them we have already noticed. They
make statements about them—statements that usually contain an "ought" or "may"—statements that

are put together, as a rule, in the form of a continuous discourse.

Continuous discourse suggests books, and that the law is in books is certainly the common impression of laymen and lawyers alike. No less a person than Langdell asserted it vigorously. Certainly anything that can be stated in words can also be written down and printed. But what is curious is that most of the statements of law about actual experience do not get into the books at all.

Not every statement made by lawyers is a legal statement. Really to be law the statements must be made by a special class of lawyers—those whom we call judges or courts. Even among these statements we make a definite selection. Judges will from time to time be asked in due procedural form to answer a question like that which was illustrated in the first lecture, a question involving a somewhat exceptional situation. Ought the benevolent employer to pay the pension? Ought the passer-by to save the person in distress? The answer to these questions is a judgment. And a judgment is the one legal statement of which the legality is beyond peradventure.

But most of the discourse about law deals not with statements that the judge has made, but with statements that a lawyer imagines the judge will make. When a lawyer—a severely practical lawyer—says this or that is the law, he is forecasting the judgment of the court. The imagined judgment is as good legal stuff as the actual judgment and plays a large part in legal construction. Not only that, it is an important legal fact if the judge refuses to make any statement, for to say that the judge has refused to say anything on a particular subject is often very much the law about the subject.

We have, therefore, in the law an escape from the uncertainty and imprecision charged against the social sciences. We have an infallible method for distinguishing a legal statement from any other. It is a statement which a judge makes or refuses to make or can be contemplated as making or refusing, about any relation whatever between human beings, provided that the statement contains "ought" or "may." The most characteristic of these statements is a decision in a particular case, the "judgment" par excellence, and it is generally the final and concluding statement of a sizable discourse.

If we can always recognize a legal statement when a judge makes it, can we always recognize a judge? That, as a matter of fact, is not quite so easy. There are a number of lawyers who are indubitably judges. They are formally so designated. They are, as a matter of fact, public officials of a special kind and they are in set terms invested with the function of pronouncing judgments. There are not very many of them.

But they must accept as associates a large number of other public officials. These officials are for the most part entrusted with administrative and executive functions, but they manage to do a considerable amount of judging. Not all administrative officials have developed the power to do this, but some certainly have. They perform a judicial function when they issue statements involving "ought" or "may" and when these statements are treated by those who are unmistakably judges as binding on them, even if binding to only a slight degree. There are thousands of such officials in the United States, and many of them are either unqualifiedly judges under other titles or at various degrees of evolution into judges. But, even if only the first step in this evolution has been taken, even if it is only rarely and exceptionally that this public official issues a statement of "ought" or "may," which will have weight by the fact that it has been issued, he has become a kind of judge and his statement is, therefore, a legal one. We may call him a judicaster,[4] if "judge" sounds too pretentious, and frequently, in order to institutionalize him completely, he is called a "court."

Of the two types of legal statements, those which the judge makes and those which he can be imagined as making, the latter are much the more numerous and more important. The persons who do this imaginative forecast for us are those we call lawyers proper, though they are not lawyers in as complete a sense as the judges are. Their competence to make this forecast is based upon the fact that they are assumed to know a great deal about how judges think and how they are likely to reach their conclusions that a certain thing ought to have been done or might lawfully have been omitted.

Lawyers derive their competence in different ways. At the common law, they derive it from the fact that lawyers and judges were once brethren of a professional guild and still are that to some extent, centuries after the guild organization has been abandoned. Judges are nearly always selected from among lawyers. That is becoming true to an increasing ex-

4. Cf. "The Chancellor's Foot," 49 *Harvard Law Review*, 44–67.

tent for the quasi-judge, the judicaster, whose primary functions are administrative.

In other systems, judges and lawyers are differentiated almost at the beginning of their careers, and
the lawyers' competence to forecast judgments is
based on the tradition of a common training. In these
systems there is a tendency to declare that not what
the judge says but what he ought to say is the law.
That is, I fancy, another result of the ambiguity of
the word which in Continental languages is used for
law. It involves both practical and logical confusions.

In still other systems and in most earlier stages of
our own, the function of the judge himself was not
yet completely differentiated. Nearly all European
systems began with a magistrate who had many governmental duties and powers, extremely diverse ones
often, and continued to perform these diverse tasks
after political scientists had pointed out their diversity. All judges were administrative officials—as indeed they have to some degree never ceased to be—so
that the modern multiplication of officials who are
both administrators and judges merely repeats a historical process.

The legal statement of a judge who was not certainly or unmistakably a judge shared the dubious
and epicene character of its source. Luckily the ritual
origin of procedure—which is so emphatically a legal
manifestation—made it possible to recognize when
the magistrate-judge was making a legal statement
and when not. It was only a step till the making of
these statements was so exhausting an occupation
that some magistrates became exclusively judges and
did not have to clothe themselves in a special garb,

sit under a particular tree or in a marked-out place, or carry a scepter or some other distinguishing insignia, in order to make it clear that the statement they were about to make was a legal one.

If the lineage of the lawman proper, the judge, is distinguished indeed, that adjective cannot be applied to all the strains that may be noted in the lineage of the type of lawman who has today appropriated the general designation for himself, whom we call simply the lawyer. Some of his ancestors are noble enough, philosophic analysts of the state and society, philanthropists who protected the poor against oppression. Another strain is that furnished by rhetoricians, artists in words who commercialized their skill. That eloquence should be venal shocked Athenian and Roman Puritans alike, but venal eloquence became both a communal necessity and a highly admired technique.

This third group, if not of as high a rank as the others, is still respectable or soon became so. The same cannot be said of another group whose claims to be one of lines from which lawyers descended are unassailable. This is made up of those who intermeddled in litigation for their own profit, men who generally professed a public purpose and sometimes had one, but who also were at least as much intent on their own gain. The Athenian sycophant—a word that has wholly changed its meaning in modern usage—was of this sort, and the contemporary references to him make it hard to distinguish his functions from many later ones, performed by quite reputable lawyers.[5] It

5. Bonner, Robert, *Lawyers and Litigants of Ancient Athens: The Genesis of the Legal Profession* (1927); Bonner, R. and

is the disreputable phase of his conduct which has obscured the fact that there had ever been a reputable phase. Even earlier than the rhetor or advocate, he made a profession out of the special skill he had in matters of law. He conducted prosecutions in the hope of public reward and frequently for partisan purposes. The fact that he was heartily disliked by the men he prosecuted is not quite conclusive, but that he was on the whole a rather sorry and disreputable interpolation in the pedigree of a great profession is indisputable.

Disreputable sycophants were called delators or calumniators at Rome and calumny was made criminal. The common law knew the sycophant and calumniator as the barrator and in some cases as the pettifogger. These exclusively condemnatory terms must not blind us to the fact that they are merely exaggerations of the distaste that was at one time felt for nearly anyone who made the quarrels of other men his own, especially when he did it for profit—which is, of course, what lawyers do.

When we boast of the ancestry of our profession, its association with sovereign power and philosophic wisdom, with charity and public-spirited zeal, we should recall what the angry prophet cast into the teeth of a people that had forgotten: "Thy father was an Amorite and thy mother an Hittite."[6] The Amorite and the Hittite loom larger in public estimate of our origin than the finer strains which we may legitimately discern in it. The hallmark of the

Smith, G., *The Administration of Justice from Homer to Aristotle*, II (1938), 89–74.
    6. Ezekiel, 16. 3.

sycophant and the barrator remains sufficiently on the lawyers as a body to make it necessary to recall that what these inchoate lawyers abused is the essence of legal practice—a special skill in conducting law suits which could be gained only by making it a business to conduct them and such a business could be created only by intermeddling with other men's quarrels.

The experience that the sycophant and barrator got disreputably and directly lawyers now get by indirection. They study what was said about old legal quarrels and what was said about these statements. They study it because the judges have studied it or will study it. This material, now grown to proportions far beyond the possibility of complete survey, is the law that is in books. It is a mass of discourse of the most diverse origin and texture.

Common lawyers think of it as being composed chiefly—although not exclusively—of what are called "cases" or "reports." The body of these cases is made up of opinions which are in theory reasons given by appellate judges for correcting or refusing to correct the judgments of trial judges. Actually these opinions are fragments of loose discussion in which the judgment of the trial court is little more than a springboard. The mass of discourse contained in these cases includes history, speculative philosophy, science, economics, sociological theories and data, as well as generalizations assumed to be derived from previous actual or imagined legal statements. It is impossible to deny that any part of this material—since it is put together on the assumption that it has some relevance to the final judgment—is legal. The fact that much of the material is erroneous, or not

really relevant in spite of our assumption that it is, is
not conclusive. Not only are Coke's historical mistakes the common law of modern England, as we have
often been told, but any judge's mistakes on any
topic are to some extent law.

The material in its varied imperfection is to a
greater or less extent available to the lawyer as to the
judge. To this the lawyer adds a real experience of
his own, dependent on records and memory, and concerned not with what judges have said and written
down but with what a particular judge has done. As
a matter of fact the judge he has in mind has rarely
written anything at all and has taken little part in
that vast scholastic discussion which is the law in
books. He has been asked specific questions about the
acts of living people and has answered them. The
question he has not yet answered—the question whose
answer the lawyer seeks to forecast—may never reach
the form of discussion in books at all, and may be
answered by the judge with a minimum of attention
to the discussion in books. How he will answer will depend on the particular judge's habit of conduct and
type of mind as well as on his study and research in
the vast and unlimited field of book law.

This field, however, is not an uncharted one. There
are if anything too many charts and too many pilots.
While I do not hesitate to call this type of study
scholastic, I do not use the word in an invidious
sense. The popular picture of medieval schoolmen is
that of futile word fanciers frittering their time away
in absurd problems, as absurd as the famous Rabe-
laisian question about the chimera bombinating in a
vacuum. It is a thoroughly false picture. The school-

men were dialecticians and mathematicians. Their end was often the extremely practical one of organization in Church and State, but if they had no other end than that of ordering their ideas about life and the world, I should hesitate to call it wasted or futile effort.

The judge is required to do much that the medieval schoolman did and it is impossible to avoid some of the technique of the schoolman. And that this technique is logical is inevitable. Merely to arrange the vast mass before him is a severe test of logical method. To attempt to solve apparent contradictions, to harmonize discords, to distinguish between apparent similarities, these are the characteristic acts and terms of scholastic method and they are repeated verbatim in any more or less extensive "opinion" in the "reports."

Nor could they avoid being repeated. If book law is to be used at all, it can be used only if it can be sifted, arranged, systematized. Any other method breaks down under its own weight. The purely annalistic method of the Year Books had to be supplemented by crude classification in the form of alphabetic groupings and these in their turn had to yield to a continually revised—if imperfect—logical classification. Those who fulminate against logic here as elsewhere have forgotten that their own zeal in proving the uselessness of logic is an example of what they profess to discard. *"Tu videlicet,"* said Augustine of his Donatist adversary, *"non dialectica uteris, cum contra nos scribis"*[7]—"And you, forsooth, are you not using logic when you write in opposition to our use of it?"

7. *Contra Cresconium,* i, xiii, 16. *Corp. Scr. Lat.* (Vienna, 1909), LII, 839.

If our judge can read and remember, he cannot fail to use logic in the process, and in this part of his task he will be the better judge, the better his technique is. But if he does nothing but read and remember, he will be indifferently equipped to answer the question put to him, for this question is a matter of experience. What ought the litigants before him to do or to have done?

Whatever he is, judge or judicaster, this man whose actual or imagined dealing with human experience makes it for the nonce legal labors under a great handicap. He is the one kind of lawyer whom we try most to dehumanize. His activities are nearly exclusively legal. He is assumed to be wholly absorbed in them. In fact, it is accounted to him for righteousness that he should be so absorbed. In Continental Europe, we have seen, he was often differentiated from all other lawyers at an early stage of his career. In England, he became more and more secluded in the nineteenth century, although never completely so. And both in England and the United States, a virtue was imputed to the ideal of a monastic seclusion for the judge. Perhaps a better picture of the ideal judge in the minds of a highly respectable fraction of the profession is furnished by one or another of ancient oracular shrines, served by a priest who was never seen at all, but who from behind a curtain or through a crevice in a cave uttered responses to questions put to him.

In the United States, we do not ask this of our judges and to that extent we do not attempt to disqualify them from direct contact with the reality of human life. We may hope, therefore, that the statements they make will be statements which are at least colored by acquaintance with living experience. But, under the most favorable conditions, their contact with the particular part of experience about which their statement will be law must be limited.

First of all, the experience brought to the judge is a dead experience. And it is insisted with vehemence that, except as dead experience, he must have nothing to do with it. Whatever a court is asked to judge must in most instances be a past event, not too long past to be sure, but often several years old. If it is not past, it is in our system not ripe for judgment. The action is prematurely brought and must be brought all over again later, if it is not completely barred by the very precipitancy of the litigant.

Now the irrevocability of the past is a subject on which poets and popular philosophers have exhausted all their powers. Humpty Dumpty and spilt milk are the nursery and proverbial versions and the moving finger that will not cancel half a line for all your piety, wit, and tears is a more imaginative expression of the same idea. It was an ancient commonplace that to undo the past was impossible even for God. Aristotle takes this for granted[8] and quotes the tragic poet Agathon

---

8. Aristotle, *Nicomachean Ethics*, 1189b (VI, 2). It was a commonplace of ancient thinking. Cf. Horace, *Odes*, III, 29, 45–48.

> *non tamen inritum*
> *quodcumque retro est efficiet neque*
> *diffinget infectumque reddet*
> *quod fugiens senel hora vexit.*

It is specifically asserted by Pliny, *Nat. Hist.*, II, 7, 27; *ne deum quidem posse omnia—nullum habere in praeterita ius.*

For this alone is lacking even to God,
To make undone what once has been done.

μόνου γὰρ αὐτοῦ καὶ Θεὸς στερίσκεται
ἀγενητὸν ποιεῖν ἀσσ᾽ ἂν ᾖ πεπραγμένα.

To be sure, relativity and two-way time and Clerk-Maxwell's demon have pretended to qualify the irreversibility of events. They will have to compound their quarrel with Aristotle, the Stoic Zeus whom we have temporarily abandoned, although I do not doubt but that he will reappear before we are through. For our purposes, the past, to use an expressive if unpleasant idiom, is a dead dog.

What shall be said of an institution which, like the law, requires its ministers to do that which experience has told us is impossible, to make dead bones live without miraculous assistance, to see a second time what by definition can never be twice made visible to a human eye? A commercial agreement is made by ephemeral human beings about transitory acts and perishable commodities. It is that agreement, concluded at a time irrevocably past, which determines the judge's legal statement about the obligations and liberties of the persons who agreed. What does he know about it? He hears the testimony of the parties concerned and of others who claim to know something of the matter. He reads the documents they have signed and the letters they have written. Such things do not constitute the agreement but merely some of the impresses that the act of agreeing has made on the environment, its reverberations, its effluvia. And with the best will in the world he cannot get into his courtroom, much less before his eyes, even so much as all the impresses of all the events that went to the making of the agreement. He has no means of knowing whether those who profess to tell him what they saw or heard some time ago remember it accurately. He cannot be sure they are telling what they really remember. And he may be quite sure that they saw and heard only a small part of what was then visible and audible. Nothing at all of it is visible and audible now, even by Extrasensory Perception.

And it would do him little good if he could reconstruct a special moment of the event he calls an agreement, the final nod of consent that turned the offer into a contract. To understand fully what happened at that moment, the judge must know what needs of the individuals agreeing were served or were to be served by the agreement, what values were set by them on the services to be rendered under it and why. Otherwise he cannot properly evaluate the actions involved in terms of a really living experience. How far back in the personal histories of the men who made the agreement shall he go? If the moment of consent itself is irrecoverable, although it was a special moment, usually marked in some way when it occurred, what shall be done for those fluid events in which all moments were fused into a stream, in which anticipation and recollection are hopelessly intermingled and the course of negotiation and discussion too casual and full of irrelevant episodes to be easily recalled?[9]

The problem is even more hopeless in a criminal case, where the need for a complete reconstruction of a situation is quite imperative, if we are really intent

9. Cf. "The Permanent Problems of the Law," 15 *Cornell Law Quarterly*, 1-24.

on bringing our human experience home alive. The determination of what ought to be done in disposing of one of the agents in a crime should be based, to be adequate, on a complete psychological study of the person accused and an equally thorough sociological study of his environment. This is not meant as a *reductio ad absurdum*, but as an indispensable prerequisite for a realization of our declared purpose to obtain a complete picture of the personal relations we are to judge. Criminologists often expressly ask this of lawyers and their first criticism of the operation of the criminal law implies that this ought to be done.

Can it be done? Obviously not with our present facilities, any more than the economic study requisite for a full understanding of the simplest commercial contract can be undertaken by the courts now functioning. It is conceivable that other courts or quasi-courts might be devised to undertake such studies. Extensive studies involving economic and sociological research have, we know, been undertaken by administrative bodies and for administrative bodies and courts. And studies involving psychological research have been undertaken both by courts and for courts, as well as by specially appointed commissioners. I doubt whether any purely academic research has been more effectively and scientifically pursued than the investigations carried on by the Securities and Exchange Commission, by the Tariff Commission, by the National Labor Relations Board, by any one of half-a-dozen crime commissions—to mention only a few. The methods and resources of science have been fully exploited to find the necessary facts, to examine them, and to determine their significance.

But the utmost research and the most painstaking investigation are unfortunately not competent to revivify the past. The event—if it is a specific event in the lives of human beings that is to be judged—remains a dead fact. It is something which must be inferred or guessed at or intuited—whatever that turns out to mean. At any rate, what is judged is not there at all, and what is there is at best a plaster cast lacking in many of the characteristics of the original, especially in the one characteristic we are in search of, which is nothing less than life. Whether science can create life in a laboratory is a matter of dispute. It seems certain that it cannot do so in a courtroom.

I am taking, you notice, courts in their largest sense and treating as their normal and usual method the attempt to come into contact with human experience by careful and exhaustive scientific investigation. I have suggested that whenever a case involving the economic and social relations of two persons comes before the court for decision, the court should undertake a study of the personal and environmental histories of these persons which would somewhat resemble the study that Robert and Helen Lynd made of Middletown; and that in a criminal case it would be a criminological study as documented as a psychiatric case history which could be appended to a book comparable to Hooton's book on the American criminal or the Gluecks' study of delinquent children. I think I shall not err on the side of overstatement when I say that this will not be found quite practicable. We can assume that a court preparing to pronounce a legal judgment will not go quite so deeply as that into all the factors of the relationship to be judged. And yet, if it did, the acts and events of the many people involved would still be past and, therefore, dead; and if the judgment of "ought" or "may" is to be applied to the living human persons then before the court, on the basis of even such monumental and accurate research, it would still be a judgment of the quick by the dead, or rather by means of the dead.

There are very few Lynds, Hootons, and Gluecks on our bench, men with the trained capacity to undertake research of this nature. And if there were, they would have at their disposal neither the means nor, above all, the time to undertake such research. Judgments must be pronounced speedily. The Constitution assures us of our right to a speedy trial when we are accused of a crime, and the investigation demanded is a leisurely process. And in civil cases also, delay is a major defect in the law, an ancient abuse against which laymen have cried out for millennia. Most cases will certainly be judged without such an investigation. More than that, the litigants are usually required under penalties and by strict rules of limitation to present to the court only a very small portion of the matters that they would like to present. Not only does the court not desire the entire case history of the acute social inflammation that it is asked to treat, but it will not glance at anything but the last few entries on the fever chart.

That is to say, the court selects from the dead past a few elements and proceeds to construct—so far as it thinks construction necessary at all—a background against which it will judge the relation of the litigants. Those of us who like may think of Cuvier and his mastodon—was it a mastodon?—accurately anticipated before discovery, from a single vertebra. Local patriotism and a now-incurable habit of irreverence might cause me to prefer Mr. Brown of Calaveras and the bones from which he reconstructed an animal that was extremely rare, as described in Bret Harte's poem. I say nothing of the deplorable results which Mr. Brown's scientific enthusiasm produced in the Society upon the Stanislow, except to point out that two reconstructions based on the same data are often widely different from each other.

To make these reconstructions of past events identical with the complex of experiences which occurred when the events took place, would be impossible even if all the resources of science were employed to perform the reconstruction. In the case of a court which has not all the resources of science at its disposal, there can be no pretense at a complete and faithful picture of the reality that has irretrievably disappeared. Why does the court make the attempt at all? Why is it not satisfied with a single indicium, an amulet, a mark, and determine its judgment on the presence or absence of this mark?

There was a time, not too long ago, when the task of the court was much simplified. A ritual, an ordeal, a hieratic battle, a phrase solemnly repeated in precise words and tones, with the use of fixed gestures, an oath—these were the things which courts were asked to determine. Their work was easy. Was the amulet or mark there? Was the ritual accurate as wise men remembered it? Was the oath taken in the proper form? This is far easier, clearly, than attempting to reconstruct the past. Indeed, it might be said that there was nothing past or dead about it. It was something happening then and there before the judge's eyes.

But this upon examination turns out not to be true at all. The ancient, medieval, and modern court that relies or relied on ordeals, amulets, and rituals—and we have demonstrably not ceased to do so altogether —had formerly a lighter burden to bear than a court that is not permitted to rely on them, but it would be a mistake if we took this lightening of its burden as indicating a different conception of the function of judgment from that of courts with nonritual procedure.

The most primitive court, while it was asked merely to determine the correctness of a present ritual, was in fact as much concerned with the reconstruction of a past event as the most modern court supplied with all the apparatus for rigorous scientific research. The ritual was devised to make certain that the past event had taken place. The possessor of the disputed article had obtained it by gift or purchase, not by theft. The accused assailant had not struck the blow. Or the contradictory of either of these things. The correctness of the ritual was linked by the intervention of supernatural powers with the happening of the past event.

And, as a matter of fact, so far as the event was a single or a simple one, the supernatural intervention was quite real. In an age of fear of demonic vengeance the ritual worked, so far as those who engaged in it could remember and restate what had happened.

Numerous stories are told which seem to prove that a person who believed himself to be an offender either declined the ordeal or broke down under the psychical stress induced by it. When the fear decayed, the efficaciousness of the supernatural linking of the present ritual with the past act rapidly disintegrated as well, but what took its place, witnesses, documents, persuasive oratory, histrionic display, supplemented slightly by the beginning of a scientific investigation—the whole complex we designate as proof—has not changed in its essential function. We must link a present and observable procedure more or less arbitrarily with a past and nonobservable event. Alas, we must do it nowadays without supernatural assistance —at least without open and admitted recourse to supernatural assistance, except in the Executive Chamber of the State of Michigan.

Lawyers and courts have been long aware of the nature of the task before them. And they have never given up hope that they might once more find the supernatural link that was broken so long ago. Trial by ordeal, by ritual, by Mumbo Jumbo, crops up frequently enough under other forms. If we may believe the stories and plays that disclose the secrets of jury rooms, trial by jury often contains all these methods in different degrees of saturation. As far as trial by battle is concerned, the lay public loves to consider a trial as a "battle of wits," and would probably resent in any case that aroused its interest an objective and careful scientific study of the data. Lawyers are even more insistent on according their technique a great deal of the character of a battle. Metaphors derived from battle are almost as numerous as they were in

56 *Law as Logic and Experience*

the *legis actio* procedure of the Roman law which was a mock battle.[10] "To give and ask no quarter," "a doughty antagonist," are phrases that suggest what lawyers think they are doing.

More even than the words they use is the attitude constantly insisted on, that the judge is to be merely an umpire in a contest in which each side is to be permitted, within the rules of the tournament, to fight in its own way. This attitude is carried even into appellate courts where lawyers resent anything which seems to give an "advantage" to either side. Interposition by the judge is deemed an interference. We should scarcely guess from the wails of unsuccessful pleaders or counsel on appeal that the purpose of either part of the legal procedure was anything more or less than deciding between two champions.

Whatever may be the continuing influence of ritual and ordeal in trials, it is of course the case that this influence at present is consciously repudiated. The court asserts and the community, despite its love of a fight, would tolerate no other assertion, that the connection between proof—that is, the observable and visible conduct of the litigants and their assistants before the court—permits by more or less irresistible logic an accurate inference about some at least of the events—and they are promptly characterized as the most important events—which took place at a definite time, days, weeks, months, or years before the trial.

We reach, therefore, our human experience by a purely logical, or mathematical, method. And we keep quite within the legal tradition, the legal process in

10. Aulus Gellius, XX, 10; Cicero, *Pro Murena*, 12 *seq.* Poste's *Gaius*, IV, 13.

general as it is the judicial process in particular, by arguing backward. One witness has contradicted another. The former has probably lied, because he is the sort of man who would lie as evidenced by certain indicia of appearance and conduct, and the other is not that sort of person. We accordingly eliminate his testimony on this point as a means of reconstruction of the event we are in search of. But we should not delude ourselves into thinking that we are doing anything else except following a mathematical formula. We know that the margin of error in our major premise is so great that it really ought not to be used at all, yet we are prone to state it as though the margin of error were slight or even nonexistent.

Before we get very far we find that we have a whole series of rules that determine the way in which we shall move—always backward of course—from what goes on before the court to what has gone on some time before. These rules are quite clearly postulates and definitions and common notions, indistinguishable from those of the first book of Euclid. We have learned within the last century that these definitions in Euclid are arbitrary. Equally arbitrary, of course, are those in this legal-logical system of ours. And there can be no doubt that the latter are more arbitrary, if we may have degrees of arbitrariness, by which we mean that the common source of both, the limited and qualified experience of a few technicians, is much more carefully generalized in Euclid than in the law.

The rules we have been speaking about are called by lawyers the law of evidence; and the common law of evidence—our law—has been subjected to violent attacks because of its peculiarly arbitrary character. The name of Bentham is especially associated with the most virulent of the attacks. Two books of his, the *Rationale of Judicial Evidence* and the *Book on Fallacies*, both edited by pupils and disciples, contain torrents of eloquent abuse against the absurdities and irrationalities of the methods in use by the courts, methods which the courts have required themselves to use by the establishment of a law of evidence. The objections, you will notice, are technical and logical— "irrationality" and "absurdity" are both logical words—and have been met by discovering irrationalities and absurdities in the objections as well.

It is, however, extremely likely that if a technically precise system of logical rules were devised for proceeding from evidence to the facts sought to be proved, our sense of being surely in possession of these facts—always remembering that only a selection of the relevant facts is possible or attempted— will not have been greatly enhanced. Our definitions and postulates will still be arbitrary even if handled with greater skill than we now handle them and the likelihood is great that the dead and static picture of the experience we seek will not even be entitled to call itself that. It will not be a picture of experience, but a diagram.

The best reason we have for thinking that our arbitrary and irrational law of evidence is not much worse as a means of imitating Clerk-Maxwell's demon and viewing the past as though it were present, than a system which repudiates our rules, is derived from the fact that foreign systems do not have these rules and still suffer from the same defects. The principle

of "free evidence"—*freie Beweiswürdigung*—is generally in vogue in Continental Europe. That is to
say, the objection to evidence as "incompetent" or
"improper" or barred for the reasons that play so
large a part in our system, may not be raised at all or
raised as we raise them. But the objection based on
"relevance" remains, which means that a set of arbitrary logical rules—necessarily varying a good deal
from court to court and from judge to judge as with
us, are applied and the direction of our movement
into the past pretty well limited by them. Again,
rules of the weight of testimony depending on personal and social rank were and are applied with a
definiteness unknown among us, and the final result is
merely that the postulates and common notions are
different but quite as arbitrary. It may be noted that
side by side with the common-law lawyer who in a moment of candor declares our law of evidence to be a
means of preventing access to the truth, we may find
more than one candid civilian who thinks of the rule
of "free evidence" as leading to anything except the
truth.

And, all the while, let us remember we are not looking for the truth at all, but for merely a shadow, a
simulacrum of the truth, a plaster cast of it in which
the conjectural restorations of incomplete fragments
are necessarily more numerous than the plausibly
accurate reproductions. And what I have sought to
point out in what has gone before, is that even this
simulacrum, this plaster cast, seems beyond our reach.
In the abstract, rules of mathematics could perhaps
give us four of the seven or eight dimensions in which
we live—time being one of them. In practice we must

at once rule out the temporal dimension, since the past is irrecoverable for us who are not relativists or demons. And if we attempt to get three dimensions, we discover that our figures, while perhaps three dimensional, are not solid but hollow. We have, not the thing, but the outlines of it, and these outlines since they are found by following mathematical rules, are not based on what happened—which we are supposed to seek—but on what is happening, the actual events and circumstances of the trial.

For mathematics, here as elsewhere, proclaims its fundamental characteristic. It will not move from its starting post, whether you seek to go forward or to go backward. Since you must begin with what is presented, all you will get at the end is another picture of what is presented, an enlarged picture, of course, but containing nothing you had not already seen. The postulates and common notions of Euclid were not invented by him. They came as a matter of fact from real experience, the experience of surveyors and engineers who in Egypt, Babylonia, and Greece had to build bridges, sail ships, construct pyramids, and erect temples, and who had to teach others to do so. They did so by making pictures of the things they did and had to do, and by generalizing these pictures until they took on the geometrical forms with which we are familiar. Once they had their pictures, they played with them, with or without a practical end in view, but they never quite forgot the practical and experiential origin of their symbols.

It is quite true that the geometry which we use in the law has likewise its roots in experience. Why may we not use hearsay evidence? Chief Justice Marshall and Justice Story declared that it was because hearsay evidence is inherently bad evidence.[11] We may be sure that when anything is called "inherently bad" or "inherently good" it is because no real reason can be found for it. Lawyers, however, had a closer approach to a reason. It was bad because the person whose statement is reported is not there to be cross-examined.[12] What of it? Ah, there we have a postulate or an axiom or a common definition. Only by cross-examination can a witness' credibility be judged. Is this derived from experience? In a way. There are certainly a number of situations in our experience in which the statement of a witness after cross-examination has been weakened or strengthened. But there are also some in which it has been left exactly as it was, and some in which true statements have been made to seem false and false ones to seem true, by means of cross-examination. Which of these experiences shall be generalized and made a rule? One, we might say, that most closely corresponds to the best authenticated experience of most men. Unfortunately, if anything is certain, it is that no one has seriously attempted to investigate the experience of most men on this subject, or even of very many men. The generalization, we may be sure, has been fairly hastily made and managed to get itself accepted. Haste, however, is a relative term. A few generations may constitute indecent haste in legal development.

We may subject most of our rules to a similar scru-

11. (Marshall) *Mima Queen* vs. *Hepburn,* 7 Cranch 295; (Story) *Ellicott* vs. *Pearl,* 10 Peters 436.
12. 3 Wigmore on *Evidence,* §1362 *seq.*

tiny. In criminal law we have rules against self-incrimination and against the use of the uncorroborated testimony of an accomplice. There are excellent reasons for these rules but these reasons are not derived from the consideration that, by omitting this testimony, we are more likely to get at a correct picture of what happened. On the contrary, it is conceded that for that purpose they might be helpful indeed.

The task of the court, therefore, to do the impossible thing, to reconstruct the past, has been performed in the way in which fallible human beings much addicted to self-deception would be likely to perform it. We go on pretending that that is what we should like to do and then we proceed to spend all our energies in doing something else, that is, in constructing a wholly imaginary picture out of what is said and done before our eyes, in which picture every element is a generalization of one of the elements actually present.

The contradiction is emphasized in the common law by the historical accident of the development of the jury who were, as you know, witnesses especially selected for their knowledge of the past event or of materials from which the past event could be reconstructed. On the Continent, the ancient rule prevailed —after a certain recession in Rome—that the judge might not go outside of what was presented to him in the courtroom. He must decide *secundum allegata et probata*.[13]

The ancient judge in fact was relieved of much of

13. Cf. "The Conscience of the Court," 48 *Law Quarterly Review*, 506–520.

the onus of making the impossible attempt I have described. He determined merely that the procedure was
correct. The burden of establishing what happened
was upon the consciences of those who testified and on
the efficacy of the divine interposition. We remember
the story of Naboth's vineyard, which King Ahab
coveted. "And there came in two men, children of
Belial, who sat before him, and the men of Belial wit-
nessed against him, even against Naboth, in the presence of the people, saying Naboth did blaspheme
God and the King. Then they carried him forth out
of the city, and stoned him with stones that he died."[14]
In this instance the sin of his death is on the perjured
witnesses and their instigator, the wicked Jezebel.
The judges who knew Naboth's innocence had no
guilt on their conscience. Indeed the famous rule of
plural witnesses is almost a mandate (Deuteronomy
17. 6) : "At the mouth of two witnesses or three witnesses, shall he that is worthy of death be put to
death; but at the mouth of one witness he shall not be
put to death." We have taken this rule into our Constitution[15] in cases of treason, and the Body of Liberties of Massachusetts Bay, the first American code,
made it a general rule for all crimes, but the notion
of witness had changed.[16] If two witnesses testified, so
far as the Biblical rule was concerned, the judge had
no choice but to pronounce sentence. The blood guilt
was not his if the man was innocent, but that of the

14. I Kings, 21. 13.
15. Article III, 3.
16. *The Book of the General Lawes and Libertyes concerning the
Inhabitants of Massachusetts*, Cambridge 1648 (repr. from copy in
Huntington Library, 1929), s.v. Witnesses (repr., p. 54).

witness.[17] This also is the special point of the Ninth
Commandment. The false witness was a far greater
evildoer when he was the chief agent of the condemnation. It was something of a paradox when popular
morality attempted to hold the judge responsible, as
in the famous story, as old at least as the first century, in which the judge is placed in the dilemma of
deciding on the proof offered and thereby condemn-
ing a man whom he knows of his own knowledge to be
innocent.

In those cases, the point is very clearly made that
by legal theory the situation as constructed out of the
evidence presented—the *allegata et probata*—need
have no relation whatever to the situation as it might
be supposed to have existed. In our present practice
a relation between the two is insisted upon but the
mathematical likelihood of an identity between the
construction and the reality is so slight that it seems
curious that the pretense is not abandoned.

If we abandoned it, should we have to go back to
a still greater use of ordeal and ritual? It does not
quite follow. The effort to reach human experience,
whether pursued by ritual or by logic, would in any
case have led only to a dead experience. The experience which Holmes preferred to logic was a living
one. Perhaps we can look for it in another direction.

17. Cf. *St. Thomas Aquinas,* Summa Th., Secunda Secundae, 64,
Art. 6.

III.

THERE is a story about an Ameer of Afghanistan who rendered an extraordinary judgment in a case. I say "there is a story," although I sometimes fear I have made it up because I cannot find where it came from. But at any rate it is like other stories about Oriental potentates for whom the Ameer of Afghanistan may well stand as a symbol. These Oriental potentates are all much alike in stories.

According to the story, the Ameer, while riding about his domain, was approached by two of his subjects who duly prostrated themselves before him and demanded justice. There was a field between their properties to which both laid claim. Each produced genealogies, deeds, witnesses, and heatedly asserted his own rights and the injustice of his opponent. The Ameer listened patiently throughout the long and noisy dispute and then asked one, "Have you a son?" He answered, "Yes." And turning to the other he asked, "Have you a daughter?" And when this was also answered in the affirmative, he said, "Then marry the young people to each other and give them the field as a portion."

The story goes on to say that there was an Englishman present who was with the royal suite on an official mission. He inquired, "Suppose they had been unwilling, Your Highness. What would you have done?" "In that case," replied the Ameer, "I should have hanged them both and confiscated their lands."

I do not believe this story. But it must be allowed to point a moral since it was obviously invented to do so. The moral seems to be that when the law is called upon to deal with a problem in which two litigants assert mutually contradictory claims, it may do one of three things. It may please one of the two and displease the other. That is our method. Or it may attempt to do as the Ameer did, please both to a less degree than either desired. Or else, it may do what the Ameer declared he might have done, if provoked, please neither but increase the public exchequer.

Now, there is no logic or mathematics in all this. There is no attempt to work backward by fixed and arbitrary rules to a result impossible to attain. What the Ameer had before him was the fact that the relations of two persons—or, under Afghan conditions, two families—were disturbed. The disturbance it was his task to adjust. And the basis of the adjustment was not the restoration of the *status quo*—or to give the phrase its complete form the *status quo ante bellum*. Not only was this *status quo* irrecoverable because it was past, but, as is most strikingly shown in international affairs from which the phrase is derived, the fact of the dispute had itself profoundly changed the relations of the parties. All that the restoration of the *status quo* would do, if it were possible of accomplishment, would be to reproduce the conditions that led to the dispute.

The Ameer, accordingly, with that profound wisdom and insight which characterizes Oriental potentates in stories somewhat more than it does in verifiable history, had no interest in the *status quo ante*, but a great deal of interest in the *status quo post*. He desired to turn an obviously unsatisfactory situation into one that might produce more satisfaction, or, shall we say, into one from which less dissatisfaction and disturbance would arise. To know whether his solution achieved this result depends, of course, on a knowledge of Afghan sociology and psychology, on which subject the Ameer may have been a highly competent expert. It is not so certain that in Middletown two hostile neighbors would become friends by being made reciprocal fathers-in-law of the same family. Perhaps they would in Afghanistan.

Our law—the modern common law which is one of the developments of the law of Western Europe—is not unfamiliar with the idea of readjustment as the purpose of judicial administration. We may speak of this, carefully crossing our fingers to avoid the evil omen, as the policy of appeasement. Greek and Roman and Egyptian law had a method by which one could ask, not for a precise award determined by a past and dead situation, but for a smoothing and correcting of a difficult and very much alive situation. The adjustment of boundaries, the apportionment of shares in an inheritance, and the taxation of damages were situations in which the Greek or the Roman *arbiter* might be called in, and enjoined to distribute property rights in such a way that while no one got everything he claimed, all who were equitably entitled at all got something.[1]

1. *Digest 4, 8; Cod. Just. 2, 55 (56)*. Bonner, R., and Smith, G., *The Administration of Justice from Homer to Aristotle*, II (1938), 97–116; Wenger, Leopold, *Institutes of the Roman Law of Civil Procedure* (1940), tr. by O. H. Fisk (rev. ed. of the *Inst. des röm Prozessrechts* [1925]), pp. 337–339, with the books and articles cited on p. 337, n. 1.

This, of course, could be made to depend on the past, quite as much as the question which engaged the ordinary action of the magistrates, and be so administered as to involve the ordeal-oath-ritual hocus-pocus of procedure which the magistrate was compelled to use or to pretend to use in order to do what he knew could not be done. But arbitrament might be and often was based, not on the past at all, but on a forecast of the future. How shall these persons be induced to live peaceably together in the future, those about whom we know that they have not managed to live peaceably together in the past? That is certainly a different problem from the attempt to find out just what had occasioned their mutual irritation and to evaluate the greater or less justification of the conduct of the participants in a past quarrel.

I have allowed a little word to slip in, which I hope you have not noticed, because I intend later on to say more about it. It was the word "equitably." It is a difficult word and we shall see it used in senses that can be placed on neither of the two coördinates of reason and experience that we have so far examined. But it can also be used in a sense in which it is almost the equivalent of "reasonable" and so has a calculable connection with the line of right reason. When an arbitrament rather than a judgment is asked for or offered, it is already a tacit admission that both have some claim—some reasonable claim—to the disputed article or position. Neither is an intruder. A complete outsider may properly be cast into outer darkness, or perhaps into a place even more unpleasant.

This presupposes that the opposing claimants know that there are two sides to the claim and are half ready to make concessions before they assert—violently and aggressively enough—that their contention is the only just one. The situations listed in which arbitration was usual often imply a moral background of this sort by their very nature. But even without this half-conscious assent in advance to some form of redistribution, some form of readjustment, there are situations in which, against the wishes of the litigants, an adjustment on the basis of the future rather than of the past is clearly indicated.

I have in mind the type of litigation which occupies a disproportionate share of the time and attention of the trial courts of the country. They are called suits for negligence and have gained their present importance by reason of the great increase of power-driven machinery during the nineteenth and twentieth centuries. We cannot live with these formidable contrivances of steel and steam and gas and electricity with complete safety to life and limb, and life and limb are frequently lost by means of them.

In most instances these injuries could have been avoided if both parties had been completely careful. The situation in which a person who himself exercised the utmost care is injured by another person who exercised no care is an extremely rare one. In popular speech as in fact, injuries are caused by "accidents," i.e., by things that just happened. It nearly always is the case that all persons concerned had to a greater or less degree failed to use some precaution.

When these accidents are examined in court, the theoretical approach is to determine exactly what happened at the moment of occurrence. When we know this, we must decide whether one of the two has been quite careful, and the other careless to some degree. Only if we can be sure of that, may we say that a wrong has been done and that the wrongdoer ought to pay damages. If both have been careless to any degree, although the carelessness of one is less, much less, than the other's, or if neither has been careless at all, no damages will be owing.

Two automobiles have crashed into each other. Just what did the two drivers do which they ought to have avoided or to have done differently? What did they omit to do which they ought to have done? The duties for the most part are admittedly impossible to put into set rules. They vary—they must vary—with the circumstances of each accident.

Therefore, in order to determine which of the two failed in his duty in that crisis, we should ask of both the drivers, first an accurate statement of exactly what took place at the moment of collision, with all the details or at any rate as many as possible. Neither driver was, we may assume, a trained observer. The accident was almost surely quite sudden and unexpected. Further, it was brief, so that when attention was directed to the collision, the whole thing was over before either man could collect his wits. Again, the accident itself, especially if it was followed by bodily injury, was a nervous as well as a physical shock and largely incapacitated the men for careful observation. And finally, so far as the facts can be recalled, they are bound to be reorganized by the memory, because each person knows what the implications of carelessness are. The motive to put a self-serving color on the story—both consciously and subconsciously—is powerful indeed.

But we are not yet quite through. Only if a man did less than he ought, can he be made to pay damages. Since what he ought to have done depends on the particular circumstances of every accident, we impose on him the task of determining what his duty was and of doing it with lightninglike rapidity, in a moment of special emotional stress. This seems rather harsh. I am fond of the story of St. Francis de Sales who was a gentleman as well as a saint and, as became a gentleman, walked about with doublet and cloak and sword. Being set upon one night by three armed ruffians, he rapidly reviewed all the situations discussed by learned casuists under which a man might kill in defense of his own life and came with equal rapidity to the conclusion that this was one of them. Then, and not till then, he drew his sword and dispatched all three.

Certainly this is a great deal to ask of men who are less gifted, less learned, and less skillful. And when we remember that this feat of casuistry is to be added to coolness and accuracy of observation and a complete disinterestedness in circumstances in which by general experience men are not cool, accurate, or disinterested; and when all this is imputed to the ordinary run of human beings in order to attempt to establish the picture of a past situation which almost never occurs, certainly we may wonder whether the Ameer's method, our Ameer who disregarded all that happened before the moment of judgment, has not merit.

We have definitely given over the reconstruction effort in the case of industrial accidents. Almost everywhere in the United States we have passed

Workmen's Compensation statutes, of which the central notion is that all injuries that occur in the course of industrial labor are within limits to be made good. There is very little consideration of how the injury was produced—there is some, of course—but there is a great deal of consideration about whether it was produced and just when and to whom. The impairment of the bodily integrity of the laborer is the primary fact and it is a present fact—or so recent that it is extremely probable that the impairment did take place. That can generally be conclusively proved, since it usually is a continuing condition.

Is there any special reason why all the situations like this cannot be dealt with in this way? The question is not the practical question of effectiveness, nor the impractical question of justice. We shall not concern ourselves with justice until we are nearly through with our entire examination. What I am concerned with here is merely a matter of the process of the law, the process which works so curiously and ineffectively and attempts so pathetically and confidently to do the impossible, when it might apparently really move forward in the direction of a possible goal.

Now, in the matter of injuries caused by negligence, the Ameer might have been a little astounded to learn that by our law, when collisions occur at sea, there is a disposition to find possible what is considered impossible when collisions of automobiles or of trains, or of human beings with trains or automobiles, occur on land. The damages in collisions at sea are divided, equally divided by the United States courts, proportionately divided by those of the

Continent.[2] If, however, the collision is due to "inevitable accident" or if the fault is "inscrutable,"
then there is no recovery at all. Inevitable accidents
are quite rare, if we mean accidents that no human
foresight could have avoided. They are extremely
common if we mean the kind of accident that ordinary human foresight does not manage to avoid. As
for "inscrutable fault," that, the courts say—the
American courts—is the situation where fault exists
but the evidence is not clear whether the fault is
wholly on one side or partly on one and partly on the
other.

Just how inscrutable it is will depend on a great
many things, the most important being the person
who does the scrutinizing. And for the most part, we
may be sure it will be found that there was evidence
of fault on both sides.

I have listened to detailed accounts of maritime
collisions and read other accounts in reported cases
and I have marveled at men who actually believed
that they could make a picture of these events—oc-
curring often at night in waters filled with craft—
and could feel sure that this picture resembled what a
demoniacally gifted observer would have seen at the
moment of collision. Phrases like "this must have
happened," "that in all likelihood did happen," occur
over and over, so that it becomes clear that the only
result arrived at is a logical pattern, which is based

2. *The Max Morris* vs. *Curry* (1890), 137 U.S. 1, 14; Mole and
Wilson, *A Study of Comparative Negligence* (1932), 17 *Cornell L.
Quar.*, 333, 604; Robinson, Gustavus, *Handbook on Admiralty
Law*, pp. 853–864; for the Brussels Maritime Conference, cf. 4
American Journal of International Law, 121.

on human experience and could be assumed without examination.

On the strength of this pattern, declared to be established by the evidence, damages are divided. The United States courts follow the Ameer's rule. The Continental courts—and the "Third International Diplomatic Conference on Maritime Law," meeting in Brussels in 1910—apportion the fault. Lord Gifford in 1824 said this was inconceivable,[3] and it is the fashion to deride him since the inconceivable was then being done quite generally on the Continent and is now the rule even in England—*Das Unzulängliche hier wird's Ereignis*—but I think His Lordship, and His highly Putative Highness, the Ameer, could each in his own way be supported when they used the crude division of equality for the refined and subtle division of proportionate loss. "Inconceivable" is too strong a word, but that it is highly improbable that the fault has been accurately divided in due proportion and, as we shall see, thoroughly useless to attempt to divide the loss at all, is almost a demonstrable fact.

The uselessness is based on the fact that most shipowners are insured against collision damage and that, however the distribution is managed, the loss gets itself redistributed equally among all shipowners in the premiums that they pay. It does seem a monstrous indirection to go through the elaborate and complicated process of a trial in order to reach a conclusion pretty sure to be wrong and, on the basis of this, find ourselves exactly in the position we would have been if no trial had ever taken place.

3. *Hay* vs. *Le Neve*, 2 Shaw 395, Scots Law Cases.

This is a long commentary on an apocryphal decision of an imaginary judge, but it will serve to illustrate the doctrine that there is no great difference between a legal process which moves forward to remodel an unsatisfactory situation so that it will be more nearly satisfactory—and does so on the tolerably safe assumption that fallible human beings have failed of perfection in conduct and intention—and the legal process actually employed in certain common cases in the law, even though the postulates of the latter contradict the assumptions just made.

In these common cases which I have labored so much, although fault is mentioned, the failure of duty is not a vicious one. The duty is that of taking a certain amount of care. Failure in it is a venial sin, we must all hope, because if it is more than that, the best of us are in a parlous state. We might be persuaded to let the Ameer sit in cases like these in which there is no doubt that both sides have suffered and in which it is likely that neither was wholly free from error. But shall we do so where the issue is of wrong and right? Shall we tell the thief and his victim to divide the stolen goods and say no more about it? Shall we pay the hospital bill of the man beaten by a thug and supply the thug with a new set of brass knuckles because he had unfortunately lost his old set in the encounter just finished? Where issues of wrong and right are quite so clear as this, I think even the Ameer would have been less concerned in sending both litigants away satisfied. Let us observe, however, that in most instances it will do us no good to declare austerely that the victim will be made whole but not the wrongdoer. In most cases the stolen property has been dissipated and the thug is insolvent, so the victim will get little out of the judgment. But, at any rate, we will give nothing to the wrongdoer. I need hardly say that this has nothing to do with punishment of the wrong and the effort to prevent its recurrence.

So sharp a severance between wrong and right in the acts which, we may conjecture, led in all probability to the situation before the court is not the rule. For reasons that will be apparent later on, far and away the greater number of situations that come to be judged are not matters where there is an admitted thief or thug confronting his victim. The conflicts that commercial intercourse creates are often stated in terms of thief and victim, swindler and swindled, exploiter and exploited, but a full examination of all the background indicates that most of them are occasioned by economic and commercial disturbances in which the share of the two individuals is not determining.

The disputes in commercial affairs are regularly disputes between buyer and seller. They are rarely questions that involve deliberate attempts by the buyer to get goods without paying for them or by the seller to get money without delivering the commodities. They usually concern themselves with determining just what should be delivered and when, and just how much should be paid and when. About these questions the right and wrong are likely to be less clear than in the instances already quoted, although the uncertainty will not prevent vehemence of assertion.

Similarly the difficulties of neighbors about the use of a party-wall or that of villagers as to rights on village commons are matters which are often hard to adjust. The right may be clear as daylight to either side but the man called upon to settle the difficulties may find the daylight to be rather that of a dismal murky day than of a sunlit one.

Such situations seem made to be arbitrated rather than to be judged on the basis of right and wrong. But if the arbitrator is taken to be merely as a rather cheaper, less qualified and less authoritative judge, little will have been gained. The arbitrator has the same difficulty as the judge in recalling the irrevocable past and falls into the same logical snares that are inevitable when a man thinks he is going forward and is in reality standing still. There is no virtue in calling a judgment an arbitration and hoping thereby to escape the difficulties of judging.

It is quite true that the avowed purpose of arbitration is not appeasement and conciliation at all, but merely an expeditious and less burdensome method of reaching the same result as a court would reach *sine strepitu aut figura judicii*. The supporters of arbitration protest that they seek to discover which of the disputants was justified in his claim—a past justification here as in cases at law. Arbitration statutes provide that an award upon submission shall have the same effect as a judgment in law, and it is assumed it will be based on the same premises.

What is at work here, however, is that antagonism of the public to lawyers and courts which runs as a red thread through all public discussion of the law. Mere expedition could be achieved and has been achieved by regular and unmistakable courts, and in many jurisdictions can be achieved by ordinary legal

procedure whenever both parties desire it. There is
often added the assertion that in commercial arbitration there is no need of "educating the jury in the
language of the litigants." It is true that courts often
do not understand technical terms of a particular
trade, but they after all have the opportunity of
learning what they mean. The task for intelligent
men is not superhumanly difficult. And the opposite
defect that experts have also somewhat opinionated
notions about their own technical methods may more
than compensate for their knowledge of how technical
terms are used in a special trade.

But what is certainly much commoner in arbitration than in formal lawsuits is the effort—if I may
use a rather extravagant statement of an enthusiastic supporter of the method—to return the contest-
ants "to society, not only as happier human beings
but as better citizens" than they were before. I am
afraid I expect no such result from any process, with
or without the *strepitus judicii*. I shall be satisfied if
their present intentions of flying at each other's
throats are abated and a slightly new situation created within which they may learn to tolerate each
other.

The great majority of arbitrations do end in a sort
of compromise, or appeasement, whether it is openly
avowed or concealed. And one basis for this attitude
is that it is very likely that neither is completely at
fault in the situation which led to the dispute. The
other basis is, I feel sure, the uncertainty of determining just what took place in past time, an uncertainty that is not cured by substituting for a duly
elected judge a *conseil des prud'hommes*. To call the

person on the bench by his first name instead of "Your Honor" or "My Lord," does not confer upon him a power that Aristotle's god did not have.

Arbitrators had historically a task very different from that of the judge. The arbiter and the litigants were, as a rule, men who stood in a special relation to each other. They were likely to continue to be in such a relation when the question was concluded. They were members of the same guild or at any rate members of the same rather small community. It was important for everybody concerned that the quarrel, if it was an honest quarrel, should be settled in such a way that the cause of quarrel be removed. Unless quarreling businessmen are made of different human stuff from other quarreling persons, they will not be readily brought to see that they were wholly wrong and their opponents wholly right. The very honesty —honesty has been postulated—of their assertions will make conviction on this point particularly hard.

I have said that arbitration in such situations is prone to be a compromise. I am afraid the word has a dubious ring. A lofty-minded Victorian wrote a book called *On Compromise* in which he made it clear that no one must ever think of doing so.[4] On the moral questions that John Morley discussed in that book, no compromise may well be the only defensible doctrine, but mercantile disputes are not quite on this plane. A compromise may satisfy neither, if we take satisfy in a strict sense, but human experience offers abundant evidence of the fact that, as soon as the first ebullition of dissatisfaction with the result is over, the basis of further quarreling is in fact often removed.

4. John Morley, *On Compromise* (2d ed., 1877).

That the arbitrator will listen as patiently as the Ameer did to the presentation of the cases, the documentation, the argumentation, is, of course, assured. But the disputants, if they have a grain of sense, will note very early that he has a damned compromising countenance. If he undertakes the task at all, he is fairly sure from the beginning to contemplate the likelihood of a compromise since, if the duel was to have been to the death, he would not have been called in in the first instance.

Mercantile difficulties are usually much more intricate than this simple case of dispute between buyer and seller. Commerce is a relation between hundreds of persons bound in a network of economic acts. Any one of these persons may become a center of such relations and nearly every one is at the same time a creditor, a debtor, a principal, an agent, a fiduciary, a beneficiary, an associate, and an officious intermeddler. If his affairs become snarled, that will snarl the affairs of a great many other persons as well. It may be necessary to liquidate his business—the word has less sinister associations in law than in politics—but if it is, it will be peculiarly hard to deal with him on the basis of clear-cut wrong or right.

When an insolvent debtor conceals his assets before going into bankruptcy, that is an unmistakably wrongful act. It may be quite proper that such a one shall go to jail or otherwise be punished as provided by law. But the debtor's misconduct may have been the last resort of a poor devil driven to extremities and pushed into insolvency by a combination of his own ignorance, the pressure of high-powered salesmen who overloaded him with unmarketable merchan-

dise, and an unforeseen shift in the public demand.
The story may equally well have been a quite different one. The debtor may have been a cozening knave
who deliberately established a credit he neither deserved nor cared about keeping, and got from poor
tradesmen goods he never intended to pay for. The
law does not distinguish between these cases. It is not
a respecter of persons, for which we have the classic
formula of Anatole France's judge[5] or the more spe-
cialized pronouncement of Mr. Justice Maule.[6]

But what we can see at once is that this is a matter
which concerns a great many people. It is no one
creditor who has been defrauded but a large group
of them. And while they are justly indignant at the
debtor's diversion of goods which they think should
be turned over to them, they are even more agitated
and apprehensive lest one of their own number should
get more than his share of the goods so recovered.

The result is the typical procedure of bankruptcy
liquidation. It was something of a tragedy for the
bankrupt of an older generation. Those who have
read Hardy's *Mayor of Casterbridge* may recall an
unforgettable picture of a meeting of creditors and
the snuffing out of the debtor's economic and social
position. American bankrupts have seemed less tragic
figures, because of the greater leniency of our rules of
discharge, but there have been examples of extreme
hardship even here, which the easy cynicism of comic
strips does not render wholly nonexistent.

5. France, Anatole, *Jean Marteau.* Cf. Cournos, J. A., *Modern
Plutarch,* p. 27.
6. Foss's *Lives of the Judges,* IX, 225; Walton, Robert, *Ran-
dom Recollections of the Midland Circuit,* I (1869), 154–156.

What happens, however, after we have disposed of the bankrupt, is to deal with what is left. We have created an elaborate system, setting forth how this dealing is to be managed. In that system there is a certain amount of attention paid to the same process of reconstruction of the past that we have in the ordinary course of judicial procedure. And when this is the main issue, the result is fairly confused.

But we do have in bankruptcy proceedings a considerable attention paid to the present and future. There is a fund to be distributed. The rules for distribution are based on questions of public policy and the general commercial welfare. Individual claimants are placed in groups designated by easily applied characteristics—there is no classless society in the distribution of a bankrupt's estate—and they receive a share which may have little relation to the question of right and wrong as between them and the debtor. Finally, we may point out that the solution which the Ameer reserved *in petto* comes in evidence early. All claims of the United States are paid in full, first.

If a degree of complexity is the mark of all business relations under modern conditions, we are fond —in the United States more than elsewhere—of making complexity supercomplex. We have not invented the corporation or company but we have used it, as the original inventors never dreamed it could be used. The structure of some corporations, with its phalanxes of common stockholders, preferred stockholders, bondholders secured by specific mortgages, debenture holders, secured creditors, and ordinary creditors, is already fairly imposing. But each one of these classes can be almost indefinitely split. There can be common stockholders with the right to vote and others who have no such right; there can be stockholders, common or preferred, each ticketed by letters A, B, C—there are only twenty-six letters in the English alphabet, but there are the Greek, Hebrew, and Ethiopian alphabets in case of necessity— and each ticket is determined by real or fictitious privileges.

If, keeping this structure in mind, we build on it a series of holding companies, parent companies, and subsidiaries, some wholly or partially inside others, and each capable of presenting a honeycomb of shareholders and bondholders such as has been described, it may be said without exaggeration that we have been looking for trouble and have found it. Then we need merely crash the whole structure into bankruptcy, and we may wonder how out of the resulting chaos even a divine *fiat lux* can bring the semblance of order.

I once entertained the hope that we might sweep away the entire mess by wiping out all types of corporate structure except the wholly independent company, abolishing all holding companies, all controlled companies, and all subsidiaries. And these companies were to have only one class of stockholders and one class of bondholders. To my great discomfiture I found that, when I proposed this literally subversive plan to the chairman of the Securities and Exchange Commission, I was called a back number and a reactionary. He would have only stockholders in a corporation, not even bondholders. I submit, however, that even my conservatism would make the problem of liquidating a modern corporation a little easier than it has usually been.

In such a liquidation, however, it is certainly beside the mark to consider what each of these intertwined groups or their constituent members did do or did not do, or intended or did not intend, at any one of the thousand moments at which they got themselves entangled in the business of one of these corporations. In a case in New York involving a pitiful small-time swindler who owned all the voting stock of a corporation, who met with himself, signed waivers to himself, passed resolutions by himself, Mr. Justice Woolsey referred to the so-called corporation in which this was done, as "this grotesque entity."[7] Almost any corporate entity becomes equally grotesque when we attempt to apply to it the constructions and geometries that we have taken as the appropriate methods of the law.

The fact is, of course, that we cannot really do so at all, and that in such a situation the method of the Ameer comes into its own. We take the property present and distribute it to those present. Unfortunately the net result is rarely satisfactory. The reason for that is that there is very little left to distribute.

I am afraid that a real Ameer confronted with the affairs of many American corporations which present themselves for liquidation would have resorted to his second method which involves liquidation in a painfully modern sense. No American, however, will approve such conduct.

7. *In re Bancunity Corp.,* 36 F. (2d) 595.

I think we can agree that while much is said in bankruptcy liquidations of proof and counterproof, the establishment of a future situation on equitable terms is much in the court's mind. This has become the particular business of the courts in a new type of proceeding that is called reorganization. The history of this proceeding is recent and well known. It arose, I venture to assert, out of corruption—the fairly infamous "equity receivership"—it attained its adolescence in the complexities of Section 77B of the Bankruptcy Act and may be said to be enjoying its early manhood in Chapter X of the Chandler Act.

Recent as it is, it has a sizable literature. Its essence lies in the attempt at the rehabilitation of a collapsed debtor-corporation, a rehabilitation which, in part, disregards the rights which were frozen into solidity at a specific moment of past time. Reorganization is interested primarily in establishing a situation out of which some dozens of groups of persons will be given a new lease of economic life, without dissipating by forcible and unseasonable liquidation the economic values previously existing.

This method of reorganization is a form of appeasement. It is hoped and expected that the various groups concerned will be better satisfied than if they secured what was "lawfully" theirs. They can, of course, be persuaded to forego what is lawfully theirs only if it can be demonstrated that this lawful claim is Dead Sea fruit. This demonstration is not impossible. Indeed, they are sometimes too easily persuaded.

The method of reorganization now practiced has one or two features that deserve notice. Among the

persons who may be consulted about it is a body of
men who have no standing whatever on the basis of
what took place when obligations arose or were
broken. That is the Securities and Exchange Commission, a curious group that perhaps embodies what
can be called the interest of the Ameer, as we understand Ameers in our country. They will be heard on
how the new arrangement is to be made.

And another group, equally without standing as to
the past events that created the difficulties, may be
heard under this system. This is the group of labor,
the labor, that is to say, which was employed by the
company which is to be reorganized. They are, of
course, vitally affected, but it is an overwhelming nov-
elty that vital concern in a new situation should of itself entitle men to be heard in court. The method of
reorganization—even before the Chandler Act—has
considered even more remote interests. In one instance
the inhabitants of a small community, which would
become a "ghost town" if the business was liquidated, were allowed to present their reasons for a con-
tinuation of it.

It is strange, but gratifying, to find that when
courts propose to establish a new relationship between
debtors and creditors, employers and employees,
mortgagors and mortgagees, they take into account
the fact that all these persons are men, that they
must live somewhere, that their living together constitutes a community, and that settled communities
have values which should not be lightly disregarded.

It is clear that all controversies between corporations—that is to say, groups of men related to each
other in a complicated and intricate way—or between

individuals, or between individuals and corporations, can scarcely be dealt with as though each were a proceeding in reorganization. But the primary purpose of these proceedings, which is the effort to render future relations between the persons affected possible and profitable, might, one should suppose, play a part in determining how any controversy is to be adjusted, not merely controversies involving insolvent corporations.

It will be remembered that the solution proposed by the Ameer involved a family arrangement. If we look at the space devoted in reported cases to family law in all its forms, under the headings of "Husband and Wife," "Divorce," "Parent and Child," we shall find a great many cases, but not as many as under many other headings. But in the feudal law, of which the older common law was a special example, family relations played an enormous part. Indeed, a separation between family law and property law was very difficult to make. Even at the present time a great deal of what we call the law of "trusts" or of "wills and administration" or of the "conflict of laws" is really family law.

The interposition of public authority in family affairs, which did not offend the feudal magnates whose collisions with the feudal king and with each other made our common law, would, we know, have offended the early Romans who thought that the *pater familias* and the family council had better manage these matters themselves. Modern society has gone back to the older Roman attitude. We do not relish the presence of public officials within the home, or at the christening.

When, therefore, our lawyers turn these family matters into legal ones by the simple process of declaring a judgment about them, they do it, as they should, with misgiving. In 1904, a distinguished commission which included not merely lawyers, businessmen, and administrators, but also scientists, artists, and writers, considered the revision of the great French Code Civil. One of the Commission, M. Paul Hervieu, urged that Article 212 be amended. It ran —and still runs—"Spouses mutually owe each other, fidelity, aid and assistance." To this, said M. Hervieu, should be added "love." The Commission rejected the proposal. It was deemed difficult for a court to decide whether husband and wife in a given case had loved each other as they ought to have done.

When courts find themselves compelled to deal with family relations, it is common knowledge that they welcome any arrangement that the parties can be persuaded to make among themselves. These people will continue to be related to each other after they leave the courtroom. Courts would doubtless like to tell them to agree in their little nests as do the birds, although I have some doubts about the accuracy of the Reverend Mr. Watts as an ornithologist. But while the judge's judgment will not make this assertion, it will attempt to establish a relationship in which agreement will not be rendered difficult or impossible by a sense of defeat or of triumph.

The futility of determining the right and wrong of a past situation in family affairs is especially illustrated in the practice of divorce. All but one American state permit divorce. All states permit annulment, which if generously applied can be made to serve the same function as divorce. But all states are formally committed to the undesirability of divorce and for that purpose have surrounded it with many procedural difficulties and have made it dependent on conditions assumed to be rare. No American state permits divorce by mutual consent.

Courts are, therefore, required by authoritative statutes as well as by their own social and religious principles to demand of a petitioner for a divorce the proof of an injurious act by the defendant, a matrimonial tort. One of the commonest is cruelty. Another is adultery. If proof of either tort is not furnished in the way required by procedure—and this proof, if taken seriously would be very hard to furnish even in the conventional sense of "proof"—and again, if proof is furnished of the commission of the tort on both sides, the court is forbidden to dissolve the marriage.

What the court does in the vast majority of instances is to take into account not what happened but what will happen. Are these persons to be compelled to have those relations to each other which they demonstrably cannot carry out satisfactorily? The ordinary answer is "No," and the court creates a very simple logical connection between this result and a situation which is not only not shown to be like the one which actually took place, but which contradicts what took place, if we take the evidence into real account. They cannot refer to public policy or social advantage, since this policy so far as declared is to the opposite effect, and organized attempts to procure a different statement of public policy have quite failed.

We do not call the determination of the quarrels between members of the same family arbitration, but unless the attitude of the courts is of the nature of an arbitrament, something that looks to appeasement, conciliation, compromise, or frankly recognizes that appeasement is impossible, their judgment will be a *brutum fulmen* if ever anything was.

This notion that the future relations of the contending parties are to be facilitated, and are not to be impeded by rankling resentments and bitterness, has always been the purpose of arbitration. The moral background of arbitration is the quasi-fraternal bond which is assumed to unite members of a single group —generally a small group. Is it inconceivable that a fraternal bond, even if of an extremely tenuous character, may be taken to unite all the members of a political community? The inscriptions on public buildings in France, and occasionally in the United States, make such a profession, and I seem to remember from my schooldays the almost disused national anthem that promised peace and safety to all Americans if they acted "As a band of brothers joined."[8] It is quite true that for some of my fellow citizens I feel only a restrained fraternal affection; but the *jus quodammodo fraternitatis* of the Roman law which determined rights in some cases did not require enthusiastic mutual devotion.[9] I should be willing to arbitrate a contractual dispute even with those fellow Americans who are personally monstrously objectionable to me.

8. It is the refrain of Joseph Hopkinson's "Hail Columbia," written in 1798 and until recently taught to most school children in the United States.

9. *Digest*, 17, 2, 63, pr.

Compromise and appeasement, it has been indicated, have bad names. Compromise has a bad name philosophically as well. It implies a willingness to surrender some part of a claim asserted as a right for the peace of one's soul and the welfare of the community. In these situations in which wrong and right are clear and definite, compromise is an impairment of right, and we may understand why by certain philosophers—the Stoics in ancient times, Kant in modern times—the slightest concession to wrong was declared to be inadmissible either on theoretical or practical grounds.

In most of the discussion on the ethical and philosophical plane which makes this severely rigid demand on us, there is a suppressed premise which only the Stoics were bold enough, or chuckleheaded enough, to assert openly. It is the Stoic paradox that there are no degrees of wrong or right, and that the slightest offense and the most serious offense must be equally avoided, lest the heavens fall and cosmos be torn asunder. So stated, its astonishing inhumanity has earned it a proper share of derision, but many ethical systems that have not ventured to be so explicit have demanded credit for lofty idealism on the basis of statements which imply just such a doctrine.

If the Stoic paradox is not accepted, the question of compromise is a matter of reason which in origin and popular acceptance, if not in ethics and philosophy, is a matter of calculation. The litigant who surrenders part of an indubitable claim to a sum of money in order to avoid the delays and difficulties of litigation has allowed wrong to triumph to some extent. He ought not to have been put to this difficult

election. But since it is impossible—or has so far
proved impossible—to devise a method of litigation
which will not involve this dilemma, we may conclude
in a proper case that the injury which the compromising litigant has inflicted on the moral fabric of the
community is relatively slight.

Von Ihering carried the doctrine of moral intran-
sigeance to a logical limit in his little book called *Der
Kampf ums Recht*, translated as the "Struggle for
Law."[10] He would have every claim, large and small,
litigated, and he brands those who through supine-
ness fail to do so as recreants to their duty. Kant, we
remember, thought that a failure to punish even the
slightest offender was a grave dereliction of duty on
the part of the magistrates.[11] Millennia earlier, the
Stoics had repudiated pardons of any kind.

All this is latent in Von Ihering's theory, which is
a comfortable one for lawyers. Obviously, if every
claim were litigated, there would be few briefless bar-
risters and law schools would be even more unpleas-
antly congested than they are. But what it implies
throughout is a sharpness of distinction between
wrong and right and an exhaustive dichotomy of human conduct by means of these words. Unfortunately,
we cannot derive such a sharp distinction from human experience and it is as little the inevitable result
of logical processes.

The fact that most relations of men do not involve

10. Ihering, Rudolf von, *Der Kampf ums Recht* (14th ed., Vienna, 1900), tr. from 5th German ed. as "The Struggle for Law,"
by J. J. Lalor (1875, 2d ed., 1915).

11. *Rechtslehre*, Pt. II, sec. 49 (Hastie's translation, 1881), pp.
200–201.

wrong or right at all is after all as ancient a doctrine as any other. The Stoics for all their queer little inhumanities were fully aware of it and said so, even if that definition of law of theirs which has been mentioned seems to have no room for *adiaphora*, for things neither to be done nor avoided, but which we may please ourselves about doing or avoiding.[12] But it is not the moral indifference of most conduct that is important here, but the fact that wrong and right are not ponderable, tangible, sensible objects, eternally alike, or at any rate alike for a fairly long time.

To say that all wrong and right in law as in ethics changes from day to day would give us a sense of living on a moral quicksand. Nor need we do so. Whenever we have an intense feeling of wrong, we are not willing to be soothed by the assurance that we shall feel differently tomorrow. Nor, as a matter of fact, are those situations which arouse so intense a moral reaction quite as temporary and limited as extreme relativism is likely to contend. The feeling of humane men that cruelty and exploitation practiced by the strong against the weak are fundamental wrongs, is now of considerable antiquity. It is not an inevitable doctrine, we know, and has even been called unnatural. There have been those who defended the abuse of the weak by the strong as a necessity of nature and a desirable element of human society. The history of this rationalized savagery runs from the Platonic Callicles to Friedrich Nietzsche and is now the accepted creed of great nations. It may be that the

12. Diogenes Laertius, VII, 101–103; Epictetus, II, 19, 12 *seq.;* Aulus Gellius, II, 7, 18.

cruel and exploiting god so widely adored in Germany, Italy, and Russia may displace all other gods and make cruelty and exploitation acknowledged virtues. But for most men of our civilization the rule that these things are wrongs has lasted a long while, even if it has not notably guided our conduct.

I think we can be disciples of the Stoics or of Kant or Von Ihering on matters involving such inhuman acts; that is to say, we can declare that we admit no concession to wrong, if we have in mind only the acts unmistakably marked wrong, like cruelty and exploitation. With regard to them, we need allow neither compromise nor surrender. Nor need we arbitrate the question whether the righteous may be sold for silver and the needy for a pair of shoes, even though the silver is of high quality and profuse quantity and even when the righteous are unpleasant in personal habits and unattractive in appearance.

Most situations do not come to us so conveniently tagged. The sense of being wronged is often a subjective impression, incapable of being adequately communicated because it depends on an individual's recollection of many past events and is frequently a cumulation of other impressions similarly founded on fragments of remembered and reorganized experience. To value this sense of wrong and right so highly that we cannot admit the moral justification of anything that will disregard it—even to a slight degree —is to give to an uncertain psychical complex something of the qualified eternity of the stars.

Could arbitration take the place of litigation generally? I think so, in all cases where the issue is not clearly between the abused and the abuser, the victim and the wrongdoer. Can these cases always be recognized? Certainly not always. Which means that courts and lawyers will be compelled first to determine whether the dispute is arbitrable, a matter which should not seem a curiously foreign problem to courts accustomed to deal with problems of jurisdiction raised *in limine*.   -

If this is done, will not the procedure in arbitration soon become as technical and as difficult to handle, except by technical experts, as that of the law? Evidently this is bound to happen, nor is it objectionable so far as procedure means system and order and expedition. It need never mean anything else if courts and tribunals are vigilant.

That courts have already in a marked degree become tribunals of arbitration in civil disputes, is a matter of common observation both in England and the United States. It would be absurd to assert that those who enter such an arbitration as bitter foes always leave it as sworn friends. Arbitraments when completed have been sometimes stigmatized by one or both parties as unjust and corrupt, and the peace that they declare they seek and pursue has sometimes been as illusory as other and more internationally famous instances of appeasement. But arbitraments can scarcely be as ineffective for this purpose as the ordinary methods of litigation and they will for a while at least have the inestimable advantage that they are not required to deal with constructions derived from dubiously authenticated past experience.

But if we fancy that we have at last got into permanent contact with human experience in the raw, I am afraid we shall be mistaken. When an arbitrator

seeks to determine how best he shall settle the dispute
—the honest dispute—before him, he has in most instances to convince the litigants that however personal and special the situation is, it is not wholly un-
like other situations in which each of them might find
himself.

It is, therefore, not completely the particular litigant whose affairs are being adjusted, but a somewhat generalized form of him. If the quarrel is about
a defective consignment of shoes, the arbitrator will,
of course, not deal with an abstract consignee, nor
yet with an abstract consignee of shoes, but with a
consignee of shoes who is much like the one before the
tribunal. He is nonetheless a generalized consignee,
but generalized within narrow limits of space and
time. The litigants are invited to consider themselves
as the representatives of their class, a small class,
but still a class.

Classification is a logical process. It involves a consideration of genus and species and differences. It involves the evaluation of characteristic qualities. But
it is an error to think that litigants necessarily refuse
to be classified and demand a decision that has no reference to other persons besides themselves. On the contrary, they have a lively sense of the interest of their
group and a full realization that except as members
of it, economic life is scarcely feasible.

It is by no means impossible to make the unique
persons who are clamoring for an exclusive award
yield a little if we can persuade them that their immediate demand will impair their interests as members of a group, even if that group consists merely of
themselves multiplied by successive dealings. As soon

as we are on this path, however, the risk of slipping down the incline, or, if you like, ascending it, and of reaching a pure parallelogram of a legal situation with all its terms fixed by its structure, becomes a serious matter. It is just as easy to be mathematical about a future situation as about a past one.

It seems, therefore, that even with a system of law that sets itself the problem of dealing with the situation which the judgment itself will create, it is not so easy as we imagine, to keep at every moment in direct contact with human life. It is not enough for us to say with the Ameer, "Marry your children to each other and forget who was the rightful owner of the disputed land." We should like our judgments to be capable of guiding the litigants in the case of future disputes. After all, they cannot always marry their children to each other. In our society the situation we are called upon to judge is one that in some form or other tends to repeat itself. The judgment itself is not a rule of conduct, but it is capable of being generalized into one. But it ought to be a rule without Kantian pretensions. It should not attempt to be a rule that may be set to the whole world. It is enough if it can become a rule of a small group for a brief time—*rebus sic stantibus*, and no longer.

Our judgments are subject to a question which the Ameer would not have felt it necessary to answer. Whether it is an arbitrator or a judge who speaks, he is likely to give a reason for his decision. If his judgment is reviewed, a reason must be found for it. While speech is inexact and full of many irrationalities of suggestion and coloring, it painfully tries to be rational, which is another way of saying logical and mathematical. Whether based on the past, or directed solely to the future, the process of judgment turned into discourse will follow the same development and take us farther away, at each accumulation of summarized rules, from the reality we thought to have firmly seized in our grasp.

But it is something to know what is happening to us. One of the earliest of our manuscripts of the New Testament, the Codex Bezae dating from the fifth century, has a passage at Luke 6. 4, which runs as follows: "On the same day, seeing one working on the Sabbath, he [i.e., Jesus] said unto him: 'Man, if indeed thou knowest what thou doest, thou art blessed; but if thou knowest not, thou art cursed and a transgressor of the law.' "[13] This passage did not manage to get into the received canonical text, but it is not without value for us. We must be on our guard. We cannot dispense with logic. It creeps insidiously into any determination, even if we resolutely decide we shall have none of it. We cannot state human experience except in terms of some generality which involves logic. Since, however, we know that this is so, it will be more nearly well with us if we refuse to let the generality run too far ahead of our purposes. Our purpose may well be adjustment, appeasement, the creation of feasible relations—within a society that has become competitive but that has not wholly repudiated the *jus quodammodo fraternitatis*. Such a purpose is hopelessly inadequate in a utopia in which there is no question about the validity of the rules of

13. The passage is cited in almost all collections of "Agrapha." Cf. Montague Rhodes James, *The Apocryphal New Testament*, p. 33.

order or about their application to a specific controversy. We who must make shift to live in a less perfect state than utopia cannot presume to have arrived
at generalities that will stretch so far away from the
intersection of our ordinate of logic and our abscissa
of experience.

IV.

WHEN the situations dealt with by lawyers are matters of commercial practice or the ordinary economic arrangements of ordinary people, lawyers and courts have as their principal function that of regulating in some way the exceptional or marginal cases in which a disturbance in these situations has occurred. In this limited field the law makes its own norms effective, but it scarcely ever fails to glance, if only casually, at the larger issues involved. On these larger issues, its influence is slight indeed.

So far as family relations are concerned, the law does little more than confirm or clarify readjustments of family life in specific instances. It rarely pretends to create the norms by which it judges. When the social norms are essentially hypocritical—that is, insisted upon in announced theory and disregarded in practice—courts find themselves compelled to maintain the same unfortunate moral dualism.

The process of the law is nearly always in all these functions retrospective in theory but largely prospective in fact. In family matters, it is almost undisguisedly prospective. In some commercial matters it is avowedly so, and it is becoming so to an increasing number.

It was the fashion not so long ago for theoretical gentlemen to devise formulas that undertook to give complete solutions of method even when these formulas made no pretense at establishing eternal and definite verities. Men wrote books like *A Key to All Mythologies; Prolegomena to All Future Systems of Economics*. No such single key will serve the law. If in some matters the method of adjudication on the basis of past conduct seems less desirable than some approximation to the method of readjustment, reconciliation, appeasement considered prospectively, it does not follow that a prospective outlook is always or necessarily better. Consistency of approach is a great convenience and a substantial saving of labor but human nature is under no obligation to make things easy for legal theorists, or even for practical lawyers. The difficulties before the court in dealing with a past situation as a basis of judgment I have perhaps excessively elaborated. Prospective application has advantages of a kind that commend themselves to science. It permits experimentation, which must be assumed to be dear to scientists. But there is a function for lawyers in which prospective application, while highly important, is less important as a form of legal activity than a reference to the past.

What we call criminal law in English and what is called penal law in French and German, is a branch of the law that common lawyers are not fond of. It is, however, the specific kind of law with which in the popular mind lawyers are most associated. In fact, law itself means in popular imagination a criminal trial, a prison, or an execution.

Now, so far as criminal law is penal law, it really should not be the business of lawyers at all. The judge was once an undifferentiated judge-magistrate. It was part of his function to keep order, to punish crime, to enforce the police regulations, just as it was to state what two persons before him ought to have done or might have left undone in some social and economic relationship. It is unfortunate that when the latter function was differentiated and assigned to professional lawyers, it was not completely differentiated and that the lawyer retained any part of the task of policing the community.

The retention of this police task has worked badly. The expert in the kind of applied ethics implicit in the framing of judgments of "ought" and "may" is rarely equipped for the other task at all. The maintenance of order, the detection of offenses, the disposition of the offenders, the protection of person and property from violence—all these call into play capacities of a particular sort. The man who can do these things well is of a vastly different type from the lawyer. It is only the accident of history that has put the two together.

That lawyers have not handled this part of their business well may be admitted. It is certainly not their fault, since they never took any particular pride in this portion of their work, although it may well be that until recently they performed it as well as any other group in the community could have done.

But since we are gradually evolving a science of penology, it would be desirable if the lawyers transferred to penologists, just as soon as they can be recognized as such, as much of the business of police as they can get off their hands. It will probably take generations after this is accomplished to make any change in the popular identification of "Law," with the sheriff or the policeman, but the segregation in fact may rid lawyers of any duty to profess being anything more than what they are. They cannot really instruct men how to conduct themselves so as to live blameless lives. They are not responsible for good order. They do not protect society from its enemies. They are simply experts in helping those whose social and economic relations with specified individuals become disturbed to adjust their difficulties in a special way.

There is, of course, another way of solving the difficulty if it turns out, as it probably will, that lawyers cannot after all completely rid themselves of the burden of their connection with crime and punishment. Lawyers—some lawyers—can definitely become penologists as well as lawyers. Or else penologists, at any rate some groups among them, may be required to be lawyers. This comes to saying that penology may be so organized as to demand legal competence as one of the elements of its training. But, in any case, lawyers who are penologists will have to abandon the ordinary practice of law and will become exclusively penologists. These problems of public order and safety cannot be dealt with as a casual and incidental matter in the technique of adjusting economic disturbances through the machinery of courts.

But even though lawyers manage to disburden themselves of a large part of what may be called "penal law," they will not be able to dissociate themselves wholly from all connection with criminal matters. Nor should they seek to. We cannot after all rely wholly on penologists. The term suggests to us kindly and humane persons in horn-rimmed spectacles, earnest in their attitude and irenic of disposition. But it must also continue to include the group now represented by policemen and sheriffs.

Even if in a future and distant age sheriffs and policemen become undoubted penologists, it will always be necessary to segregate the man who places a robust hand on the collar of a thief from the man who determines what in the interest of society—and of the thief—should be done with him. This former sort of penologist will be a definite type—we may call him Class B penologist or by any other designation. And this secular arm of penology, these Class B penologists, will, I am afraid, always be the arm of men who cannot quite be trusted with unlimited discretion over the persons of their fellow citizens.

The vast majority of persons who are arrested by policemen, arraigned before courts, sentenced, and punished, are men who are definitely punishable within the rules of order of our community. But there are always a certain number who are not so punishable and who are nonetheless arrested and arraigned and come thereby in imminent danger of being sentenced and punished.

We are committed to a system of society in which this danger is to be reduced to a minimum. Freedom, in fact, means that this danger has been so reduced. It cannot be completely eradicated. But we cannot even reduce it unless we keep a careful watch on the secular arm of penology before it is heavily placed on the shoulder of a person assumed to be punishable.

Can lawyers, who have not proved to be very good at the task of dealing with punishable persons, be entrusted with the task of preventing the punishment of nonpunishable persons, or that of preventing them from being placed in jeopardy of punishment? I think they can. And I should say they ought never to forego the responsibility of assuming this task.

There are several groups of nonpunishable persons who are likely to be put in jeopardy. One consists of the lowest economic group, the persons who have obviously not made good and whose failure may be due to moral and personal deficiencies as well as to economic accidents. They are, as the President has said, ill housed, ill fed, ill clothed. And they look it. If the orbit of their activities brings them within the range of a crime, they are the immediate and natural suspects.

How much of this is due to the feeling that persons for whom the social structure has found no comfortable place are likely to have no special love for it, and how much is due to the touch of brutality that may be indispensable for the performance of the first step in the police function, we need not examine. But that we are not a free people if these persons, already ill dealt with by the community, are prejudiced in their freedom because of that very fact—this, I think, should be clear. Lawyers as judges and lawyers as advocates and, I make bold to assert, lawyers as prosecutors, cannot be better employed than when they enforce with care and persistence the rules of "ought" and "may" as applied to policemen and sheriffs. Policemen and sheriffs, I suppose, are not improperly symbolized by the figures, called *Kratos* and *Bia*, "Force" and "Might," who drag Prometheus to the rock in the prologue of the ancient Aeschylean tragedy.[1] And lawyers must be particu-

1. *Prometheus Bound*, 11. 1–87.

larly on their guard when, instead of a Titan, the persons dragged off are bedraggled members of the economically submerged classes.

Another class of nonpunishable persons who are only too likely to be confused with those who are punishable consists of men who hold unpopular opinions on social and economic questions. They are often not in the economically submerged class at all. Indeed, it seems that they are not submersible, in spite of extreme efforts to make them so. They are, as likely as not, well dressed and well educated. They express themselves well, far too well for their own comfort. They are, of course, nuisances and troublemakers. They disturb the serenity of clubs and the placidity of the breakfast and dinner tables of estimable people. They are out of tune, out of step, and they refuse to get into tune or step.

We have built our society on the doctrine that being out of step is not a punishable offense. Most of the great figures in history became so by being out of step, which does not quite mean that to be out of step is a mark of greatness. But there is a strong pressure on those who do our policing in the first instance—our Class B penologists—to make it so. It is not quite their fault. We may assume that the conduct which we do regard as punishable, theft, rape, murder, fraud, are things our policemen have no impulse to do. They also have no impulse to entertain unpopular opinions. It is easy for them—since they have not studied Aristotle's Topics—to regard these two categories of conduct as essentially similar. Sometimes, to be sure, their difficulty is morally less innocent than ignorance of Aristotle.

At any rate, it is in regard to persons of this class that the vigilance of lawyers—all types of lawyers—in enforcing the rules of "may" and "ought" on policemen, is equally imperative. These rules in any specific case will take the form of a definite statement by a judge and he will act—he cannot act otherwise—in a definite procedure. The difficulties of that procedure I hope I have indicated. Whether it is pure ritual or whether it is based on the most approved scientific methods, it seeks what, strictly speaking, is impossible of attainment. But I hope I have also made clear that the result, while impossible of attainment, can be approximated sometimes with relative accuracy. Our methods do not make it likely that we shall be as accurate as we could be, but our methods can be improved. The difficulties, however, are sufficiently great to make us ask in every instance whether it is worth while. And the answer may well be in civil matters—that is, in those matters which are derived from the disturbances of most economic and social relations—that it is not quite worth while, that the goal sought should be rather economic rehabilitation and readjustment, and that this goal can be achieved without undertaking the difficult and cumbersome task of making sure that a past situation is reconstructed in our minds as accurately as could be done with all the resources of scientific investigation.

If we could distinguish between "criminal" law and "penal" law, and could make the former mean the discrimination between those who are punishable and those who are not, we might say that criminal law alone is the business of the lawyer, and that in criminal law the retrospective process is essential, not for reasons of logic, but because of an experience that is attested by our history and by our daily lives. The fact that it is declared to be logical, to have the same direction for the legal process in civil as in criminal matters, is not conclusive. It is logical only on the suppressed premise that law always works in the same way, that, being the same word it must have the same function, or it must be applied in the same way no matter what its function.

The fact is that in criminal law, in the restricted sense in which I shall use it, the function of law is quite definitely not that of keeping order but of preserving liberty. Dissatisfaction with the results of a system of proof which can only approximate a scientific investigation and cannot rise beyond a reasonable conjecture, even when it is wholly scientific, will not weigh against the experienced results of a system which makes men punishable because of what they will do or might do. Such a system is incompatible with freedom and the human dignity which only freedom guarantees.

For this alternative has been tried. It is in fact the method used by Ameers. It has had supporters in all stages of communal development and still has powerful advocates. It attained consciousness and a sort of philosophic dignity in the early development of absolutism during the Renaissance, by being called "reason of state." That is to say, the punishability of a person depended not on what he had done or not done in the past but on a prediction as to whether the community would be better off without him than with him, or whether his relegation or punishment would be an act beneficial to the state.

The notion of "reason of state" is represented for us in an institution of our own law, the Star Chamber, whose infamy in history is only partially deserved and above all is not deserved for the reason usually assigned.[2] It was in no sense a secret tribunal. It was in fact as accessible and open as most of the other courts. And for a large part of its history it was what it professed to be, a tribunal of criminal equity, a place in which the small man would be heard against the great without the intervention of that machinery of clerk and barrister and sheriff and jury in which the great man by his wealth and social position had a preponderant influence. "Laws grind the poor," said Goldsmith, "and rich men rule the law."[3] It was true beyond peradventure in the fourteenth and fifteenth centuries. Criminal equity could, however, be made to involve reason of state. It could be made to assert that not the precise past conduct or misconduct of a man—although that was a relevant subject of inquiry—but the character and personality of the accused, and his utility or inutility to the community, would be sovereignly determined by the members of His Majesty's Council sitting in the Star Chamber.

The Star Chamber did not impose the death penalty. But it used torture and inflicted mutilation— both thoroughly English devices for dealing with undesirables, although they had dropped out of use in the court of the King's Bench before the seventeenth

2. Cf. "The Right to a Public Trial," 6 *Temple Law Quarterly*, 381–398.

3. *The Traveller.* The passage is generally quoted out of its context. Goldsmith is in fact deploring the growth of the Whig oligarchy.

century. It was, however, not these things nor yet the alleged secrecy but the degeneration of criminal equity into judgment by reason of state and nothing else which was the cause of its abolition. Reason of state was one thing when it was applied by the early Tudors to break the remnants of the great houses and to prevent new great houses from arising. It was quite another when it was used as an undisguised instrument of "Thorough," against the new middle class of small landowners and city merchants.

Reason of state in Continental Europe has a sinister history. The struggle against it was part of the effort of eighteenth-century rationalism. It was led by Beccaria and Montesquieu, who leaned heavily on the example of England with its supporting legend of Magna Carta; it was confirmed by the newer constructs of natural law and a revived right reason —the ghost of Chrysippus of Soli must have loudly exulted. It became formulated in the phrase *nulla poena sine lege*,[4] which every modern state until recently regarded as axiomatic. It was reserved for nineteenth-century Germany and Von Liszt to call this doctrine the "Magna Carta of the criminal."[5]

That Russia, Germany, and Italy have with greater or less frankness gone back to reasons of state as a basis of penology is an indication of the influence on Europe of our Ameer of Afghanistan—even if it is true that he is a hypothetical and fantastic Ameer. Fantastic is an epithet not inappropriate to the re-

4. Cf. the exhaustive study of the maxim by Jerome Hall, *Nulla Poena sine lege*, 47 *Yale Law Journal*, 145–193. Cf. also Lieber, J., *Hermeneutics*, pp. 294–296.

5. von Liszt, Franz, *Lehrbuch des deutschen Strafrechts* (26th ed., 1932), I, §4, n. 16, p. 25.

sulting criminal law of these countries. But since this attitude, that of looking prospectively at the effect of the sentence rather than retrospectively at a past and imperfectly recovered situation, is one for which I have strenuously argued in the preceding pages, it may seem strange that I repudiate it here.

The fact that it seems to me definitely to be rejected is a particular instance of the doctrine of Holmes with which we began, that the life of the law was not logic but experience. The logic that insists on the principle that any method used in one field of legal application must be used in all is, to be sure, a wooden type of logic or perhaps a mountain-goat sort of logic which leaps from particular to particular without much examination of the intervening generalization. But even if the generalization had been carefully enough made it would remain true—a purely pragmatic truth—that the two types of legal application must nonetheless not be subsumed under the same generalization, because of the unescapable fact that the persons who are likely to apply the law are different sorts of persons.

It is amply attested by human experience that no group of men who are likely to be entrusted with the function of policing the community—and that applies to the Class A penologists who are trained in law as well as the Class B ones who are not so trained —that no such group can without serious peril to our freedom be allowed to discriminate between punishable and nonpunishable persons on the basis of communal value. Only a system of discrimination on the basis of personal and individual conduct, demonstrated as a fact with the greatest approach possible to scientific accuracy, is compatible with free life in a humane and civilized society. The compatibility is not a matter of logic, but of experience.

We must, therefore, attempt in these matters of criminal law to do what it may not be profitable to attempt in other legal situations. It must first be made evident what the act was that is to be the basis of punishment, and it must then be shown that it was within one of the categories of punishable acts previously fixed. This would be so without logic. This sort of thing permits people to feel that they are living in a free community. Any other method, so far as our experience goes, does not. It may be different at some future time. I hope no one will attempt to find out, in any community in which I happen to be.

The former method requires, however, an undoubted application of logic. The determination of a past act must necessarily be a matter of quasi-scientific proof, a kind of proof that at best reaches an approximation and, given the defects of our tests of veracity and given the conjectural character of reconstruction of data, has to be helped out by logical patching, such as presumptions and assumptions. Then, when the constructed fact is regarded as established, we have the purely logical question of determining whether the act falls within the categories of punishable acts previously fixed.

Purely logical and yet never completely carried out according to the methods of the syllogism. Or rather, quite within the methods of the syllogism since here, as elsewhere, the immobility of the logical process is once more exemplified. Is the use of euthanasia murder? Is an operation to prevent the result of a rape a criminal abortion? The definitions of these categories can be labored until a perfect syllogism is contrived that will give a negative conclusion. Or the syllogism can be kicked aside and a negative result obtained without it—that is, really on a syllogism with a premise not derived from the categories.

With or without a syllogism, we detect the intrusion of a kind of reason of state. We begin with the feeling that the person before the court is in some fashion not to be classed as punishable. This is, of course, a conclusion, and the communal welfare, the modern version of reason of state, is the premise. That is to say, reason of state may be tolerated in a small degree if it denies punishment and not if it asserts it. And this illogical result is a defensible proposition derived from experience. But even on the side of leniency, reason of state in any form is, we feel, a device dangerous to our liberty and it must be rarely resorted to.

The simplest device for applying this type of reason of state is not the more or less difficult one of making a statement mean what it does not seem to mean, but of interfering in the method of verification of the past event. That we have seen done in divorce cases. If we deliberately decline to utilize even such imperfect machinery as we have for the reconstruction of the past, we can report our nonfeasance as lack of success. Juries have acquitted men with whom they sympathized after finding that an act had not been proved, although the evidence was overwhelming, so far as evidence can be overwhelming. The sympathies might be corrupt. In a famous ancient case, Cicero tells us it was like finding that the sun did not shine at noon. But the sympathies may be dictated by humanity and a sound sense of communal welfare.

For most matters of criminal law, the share that lawyers—lawyers proper who have not become penologists—will retain, will be that which concerns the effort to discriminate between punishable and nonpunishable persons. When it is determined that any particular persons belong in the former class, the utility of the lawyer—any kind of lawyer—is enormously reduced.

We cannot permit a decision on whether a man is punishable or not to depend on reasons of state. But such reasons may be valid enough in determining what is to be done with him. The rational century was true to the accounting origin of its Goddess of Reason in assuming that a fixed ratio could be made between misconduct and punishment, an eternally right ratio, so many years of seclusion for so many foot-pounds of wrongdoing. This was also the doctrine of Lao-tse in his treatise on Response and Retribution and has crept into other religious systems as well. We have come to doubt the precision of this method of accounting.

The nineteenth century on the Continent had much to say of the individualization of punishment. The most striking application of it in the United States is in the form of the indeterminate sentence with its attendant institution of parole and its implication of reform and rehabilitation.

It is a portentously difficult science—this nascent science of penology—and still in its infancy, although it is not as young in years as many other sciences. But it ought long ago to have been apparent that lawyers are no better suited for the mechanism of dealing with offenders than almost any other class in the community would be. Not so well suited as other classes. The imposing of a sentence by a judge, the most characteristic part of his duties in popular imagination, is the least judgelike thing he is called upon to do. He is not likely to know enough about the convicted criminal to sentence him properly and he is glad to have as much discretion removed from him, by positive provisions of unmistakable statutes, as is feasible. Those judges who enjoyed the task of sentencing were apt, like Braxfield,[6] to have had more than a touch of sadism about them, and it is characteristic that they never relished their power quite so much as when they were employing it against those whose classification as criminals is generally most dubious, the group made up of the economically weak or the group made up of social, political, or economic heretics, those who persisted in keeping out of step.

We are a badly policed community. It is quite true that we are better policed then we were a hundred years ago, or even than we were fifty years ago. But on the whole, fraud and theft and violence are somewhat more prevalent among us than they need be or than they are in comparable countries of our size and degree of civilization.

Are the lawyers responsible for this to any extent? Certainly they are charged with it by popular

6. Mr. W. Roughhead in his article, "The Real Braxfield," 26 *Juridical Review*, 165–190, proves that Braxfield did not stand on his dignity but scarcely mitigates the ferocity of his attitude in criminal cases. Cf. also "The Bi-Centenary of Braxfield," 34 *Jur. Review*, 1–31.

opinion and this charge plays a large part in the indictment that popular opinion has long drawn up
against the lawyers. The maleficent interference of
lawyers with the good order of the community is assumed to take place in the early stages of the police
process. The police seize the offender, the lawyer at
the bar wrests him from the hands of the police, and
with the connivance or stupidity or helplessness of the
lawyer on the bench, sends him back to prey on the
community.

It may be worth noticing that whether this is so or
not, it is a rather recently added count in the indictment. The indictment is at least as old as the fourteenth century in England, but successful advocacy
in criminal cases was possible at the common law only
after prisoners charged with felony—and most offenses were felonies—were allowed counsel, which was
not until well into the eighteenth century. And it was
not until the nineteenth century that counsel might
address a jury on a prisoner's behalf. It is to the
manipulation of juries that laymen ascribe most of
the harmful activities of lawyers.

We must therefore assume that if lawyers hinder
the orderly process of law as much as it is declared
they do, their unpopularity cannot be based on this
fact, since they were unpopular long before they were
given any chance of offering this hindrance. It is
hard to believe that any person would seriously prefer to the present situation that of the eighteenth and
previous centuries, when almost every crime was a
hanging matter and almost every indictment a conviction, and when the interference of lawyers in this

part of the police process was rendered extremely difficult.

It was in fact the harshness and cruelty of the criminal law that produced a demand for the lawyer-advocate and re-created in nineteenth-century England the condition that had fostered the lawyer-advocate in the last century of republican Rome. It is a further element of similarity that in England and in Rome the advocate became very much of a politician and used his advocacy as an element of political advancement. But in any case, the abuse by lawyers of their special acquaintance with courts in order to enable punishable men to escape punishment did not become the main charge against lawyers until, in the nineteenth century, a new genus of punishable persons arose, whom a late President of the United States designated as "malefactors of great wealth."

The malefactors Theodore Roosevelt had in mind were not merely respectable citizens. They were nothing less than eminent. In the following generation a group of malefactors at the other end of the social scale, malefactors of sufficient aggregate wealth to pay substantial fees, was developed in the organized gangsters whose activities are quite as much outcroppings of economic conditions as the large-scale swindling of those who despoiled huge supercorporations.

That lawyers were found who were the willing agents of these two types of highly punishable persons, lawyers who utilized the safeguards designed to protect our freedom, for the purpose of protecting those who were essentially the enemies of our freedom, is unquestionable. But that it is their skill alone which has given this group of malefactors their impunity is extremely doubtful.

Logic and experience are in marked conflict here, as far as public opinion is concerned. The power of lawyers to interfere in the police process produces a clearly harmful result. Whenever it is this particular situation that is in mind, the logical impulse to generate a large category out of it threatens to eliminate the lawyer altogether from any association whatever with police, and to surrender to the discretion of a socially rather irresponsible group of officials, not only the freedom of the relatively unprotected groups but, on occasion, the freedom of those of us whose bulwark of wealth or respectability is not wholly impregnable.

We can, therefore, not characterize the lawyer's connection with criminal matters as either bad or good. It is bad when it enables gangsters to beat a murder rap or looters of corporations and banks to bedevil judges and juries. It is good when Thomas Erskine can secure the acquittal of Horne Tooke or defend Thomas Paine with all the powers of reaction arrayed against him, supplemented by a public opinion quivering with horror at the French Revolution;[7] or when Mr. Justice Black can read for a unanimous Supreme Court the decision in the case of *Chambers* vs. *The State of Florida*, reversing the conviction of four Florida Negroes.[8] It is clear that logic and generalities will not help us, but that we shall need some

7. Erskine, Thomas, Speeches Connected with the Liberty of the Subject (1810), ii, 1–182; iv, 1–137. Ed. by J. Ridgway.
8. *Chambers* vs. *The State of Florida*, 808 U.S. 541.

change in the attitude of lawyers, of policemen, of judges, and of the public.

The public which exclaims against the technicalities of the law when habeas corpus is used to release an accused gangster, or when the rules of evidence are invoked to delay process against powerful politicians, or when a wealthy corporation magnate is acquitted by a jury, is also the public that takes its favorite imaginative exercise in books and plays which tell how, except for habeas corpus and delay in procedure and unaccountable jury verdicts, the condemnation of the innocent would be far greater than it regrettably is. In acting this way, the public is acting quite humanly, if not quite logically. If it did so knowingly, we should be better off.

For if we knew that we were doing as the man who labored on the Sabbath was asked to know, we should be in a fair way to get rid of the bad logic which troubles us when we have to give an account of our conduct, and above all troubles lawyers who are so frequently engaged in explaining to each other what they have been doing. We should be able to make up our minds whether we valued freedom and the Bill of Rights more than the vicarious satisfaction of our vindictiveness, when a crime is committed that stirs public imagination. The police official who with a fine disregard of forms and technicalities sweats a confession out of a sadistic murderer is the same policeman who with the application of calcium light and rubber hose breaks down the morale of the hero or heroine of our latest mystery novel—or tries to. The heroes of mystery novels are tough gentlemen.

Does logic require us to surrender the Bill of Rights in both cases or to allow its provisions to be abused in any case? Or does it require us to demand a test of the two types of cases, to surrender the Bill of Rights where gangsters and sadists are involved and to insist on it when persons are concerned who have the stuff of movie heroes in them? Or shall we say here that the rule of thumb is better than logic and that we can leave things as they are, because, after all, innocent persons are not often convicted and, when they are, it is a risk they run by living in the community, like being run down by an automobile or being crushed by a falling building in an earthquake.[9]

This would be a reliance on experience, a fairly raw and unpleasant experience. We may wonder whether it has not moved a little farther away from the intersection of logic and experience than it was required to do. To say that our difficulty is due to the tendency to confuse contraries or opposites with contradictories savors of the worst form of logic, that higgling about terminology which we are told is the enemy of economic and social and sometimes of spiritual salvation. Mr. Rivers, following psychological guides, has called the confusion of these logical terms a psychosis.[10] It is at all events a tempting and treacherous solution in many situations.

9. Mr. Edwin Borchard's book, *Convicting the Innocent,* might serve to remind us that innocent persons are often enough convicted in cases in which overwhelming proof of innocence can be offered, so that we may wonder uneasily how frequently this happens when the proof of innocence is somewhat less complete. Cf. "Pretense and Reality in Criminal Law," 4 *Oregon State Bar Bulletin,* 134–152 (June, 1939).

10. W. H. R. Rivers, *Instinct and the Unconscious* (2d ed., 1922).

If we choose to remember that logic does not require us to be guilty of Mr. Rivers' psychosis at all, we might ask whether we are really confronted with a parting of the ways between the use of the Bill of Rights that is likely to protect the guilty and its disuse at the risk of sacrificing the innocent. Perhaps, if we had recourse to a larger experience than that which seemed to present this choice, we might find that there was no dilemma before us.

Our Class B penologists are now impatient of the Bill of Rights—even the honest and competent among them—because in cases of unmistakably punishable men, cases which the lawyers cannot adequately deal with at all, the Bill of Rights does invite the interference of lawyers to the detriment of public order. But their impatience is based partly on the fact that in our system they have not quite been trained to be penologists. They do not know all the methods which psychology, psychiatry, physics, and chemistry offer them, methods which are quite compatible with habeas corpus and due process of law. If they could rely more on the process of science, they would have less hostility to the process of law.

To be sure, it is not quite so simple. Science in these things is itself inadequately trained, which means that no matter how scientific our police methods become, they will not be automatically effective. And some of the specific forms which process of law takes in our system are unnecessarily cumbersome and by that fact are subject to abuse. We are still using generalizations on the basis of seventeenth- and eighteenth-century experience, which the law must learn to conform to the experience of the twentieth century. We shall have once more to move back on both coördinates to our point of intersection. It is unfortunate that this point of intersection exercises a distinctly centrifugal force on us whenever we seek to formulate legal relations.

The different types of formulation that we have examined so far are superficially alike because they can all be stated in terms of "ought" and "may." Actually, however, they are as diverse as the purposes they serve. The judicial function which serves these varied purposes gradually detached itself, as has been said, from the undifferentiated activity of a magistrate who was a political administrator, a military leader, a priest, and other things, besides being a judge. How flexible the judicial function, the legal function proper, is can be seen from the fact that it can be turned back on itself historically and made to renew its connection with the political function of government.

On the continent of Europe, the separation of the governmental and judicial functions took place long before the feudal king ceased to be a legislator. The separation, indeed, became sharper and sharper and, by the complete severance of the two, the judicial office became definitely subordinate to that of the governor or prince. This remained the case when, following English models, a legislative body was created after the French Revolution.

In England, the separation of the government and the judiciary never quite reached the same degree of definiteness. There the legislative functions of the prince became more and more assigned to a council that developed into a representative assembly. The final creation of an independent judiciary. came somewhat later and the legislature had become a powerful and self-conscious institution before such independence was effected. It was the executive rather than the judicial function of government that tended to become subordinate.

These are two special developments of relations between legal functions and the general governmental functions, out of which law was differentiated. In the United States, on the other hand, the system that is called constitutional law has placed the court in a new relation to the other branches of government. The source of the American doctrine and practice is a matter that cannot be examined here, but that, at the present time, the courts of the United States have a power of interfering with legislation, which they have in almost no other community, will hardly be questioned. Other countries in America and Europe have followed this example in varying degrees, but its most complete illustration is to be found in the history of the Supreme Court of the United States.[11]

Our courts continually assert that they do not share the legislative function at all. They do so partly in order to forestall criticism and partly because they have been trained, as we all have been, from boyhood in the dogma of the separation of powers. That any court can avoid legislating is, of course, impossible. The process of interpretation of

11. The various books of Professor Edward S. Corwin are enlarged commentaries on the political and legislative function of the judges in constitutional cases. Cf. *The Doctrine of Judicial Review* (1914); *The Twilight of the Supreme Court* (1934); *Court over Constitution* (1938). The same may be said of the many articles of Professor Thomas Reed Powell.

statutes involves it. The extensive use of precedent by
our courts equally makes legislation inevitable. But
both these kinds of legislation are in theory and practice subordinate to formal legislation by the specific
institution created for that purpose.

The judicial review of legislation is of a different
sort. It is well enough for courts to announce that
they consider only questions of power and not of policy. The distinction is not always easy to make. Sometimes the existence of the power depends upon the
policy which the legislature seeks to pursue. But in
any case, it is as idle to say that it is not a legislative
act to determine whether legislative power exists as
for a court to declare that the determination of jurisdiction is not a judicial question.

Our courts—and above all the Supreme Court—
have, despite repeated and vehement disclaimers, become a third legislative house. The questions involved
in constitutional issues, no matter how vigorously
they are forced into the categories created by tradi-
tional court action, are questions of politics, as John
Chipman Gray declared they were. Certainly they are
removed almost by universes from *Littleton on Tenures* of which perfect book Gray's overwhelming five
thousand pages of *Cases on Property* may be said to
be the last and most luxuriant flowering.

Judges who pass on questions of constitutionality
must submit to being statesmen. Certainly the function they perform is not that of adjusting the marginal incidents of economic disturbances nor of
appeasing quarreling citizens nor of reorganizing
collapsed business groups. It is not even that of safe-
guarding the liberties of individuals, although when

it is a liberty of a group, as it generally is, that may be a purpose not unbecoming the activity of statesmen. When they guide legislative action, they are not merely legislators but something of the nature of elder statesmen and it is far better for them to be completely conscious of that position than to profess that they are in fact making minor adjustments of property disputes.

There is no one key to all legal problems. There is no one method. There is no one attitude. And the fact that a method is logically absurd, that it pretends to achieve something it knows to be impossible, will not rule it out when in practice it serves our human and social purposes better than a finely systematic and logically consistent method, or even than a method that is socially serviceable under other conditions. And similarly the fact that constitutional decisions use the language of adjudication does not change the fact that we have in this respect fused governmental functions on a new pattern after having taken some centuries to differentiate them.

Prospective or retrospective, logical or empirical, the lawyer's technique is applied in form to the relations of individuals. At various points in what has gone before, it is clear that even the most satisfactory adjustment of the relations of the parties before him has had to take into account the fact that these persons are not the only people concerned in the judgment.

When large corporations are reorganized or liquidated, when constitutional determinations are made, the court—which can be best defined as the law at its point of explosion—is aware that the plaintiffs and defendants who are physically present are only the first members of a procession that extends no one knows how far outside the courtroom. But even in other situations the courts are, or might well be, uneasily conscious that John Doe and Richard Roe are not alone. As in medieval law, they appear with compurgators, sometimes with a large number.

We do not live by ones and twos but in groups and each one of these groups is a creation of logic upon experience. Any one grouping cuts through and across other groupings, a fact which makes all social study so difficult. A man is a citizen, a neighbor, a Mason, a Methodist, a husband, an employee, a graduate of Public School Number 111, a customer of local tradesmen, a mechanic, a Democrat, a collector of postage stamps, a movie goer, a radio listener, a baseball fan, and a descendant of Welsh immigrants. The trouble is he is all these things at the same time and any one of these associations may help determine just how his affairs should be adjusted in civil matters and what shall be done with him if he is found to be criminally punishable. All this, however, makes him nothing more than one unique and indivisible person nor does it justify his treatment as anything else.

There are, on the other hand, certain adjustments which are peculiarly matters of group interests and in which the individual litigants are merely present in a representative capacity. A great many matters of constitutional law are of this class, particularly when the constitutionality of Federal or state statutes is in question, a fact that of itself indicates the great difference in the function of the judge in constitutional matters and his function in formulating other types of judgment. The constitutional judge is dealing with statutes and statutes are rarely directed at individuals but are often directed at groups. When the State of Oregon made attendance at the public schools compulsory it obviously meant to restrict, if not to eliminate, parochial schools, and there can be no doubt that the legislation was aimed especially at the parochial schools of the Roman Catholic Church. The particular litigant in this specific case, the Society of Sisters,[12] had the support of counsel and friends who would not have been available if it had been merely a matter of adjustment with landowners owning property adjoining a church, or if it had been a claim based on business transactions. Roman Catholics throughout the country very properly felt themselves concerned, since religious education within their Church is an important group interest.

Again in a pending California case, *Union Trust Co.* vs. *McColgan,* the suit by the Trust Company is not one that will be treated by either the courts or the plaintiff or the defense as something exclusively the business of the litigants. If the Trust Company wins, a great many California banks will receive a tax exemption, estimated at a total of some $14,000,000. It is safe to assume that other banks beside the Union Trust Company are aware of this. It is safe to guess that if the attorneys for the Trust Company need the assistance of other bank attorneys, they will get it. It is almost equally safe to guess that, before this action was begun, there was some conference between the banks concerned.

12. 268 U.S. 510.

In matters like these it is a group and not an individual whose affairs are to be regulated. But, in both instances, the representative character of the individual litigant is a *de facto* one. Even if he had no such representative character he would nonetheless be present as a plaintiff. He has an immediate and not merely an indirect interest in the outcome of the litigation. The group is really only a multiplication of the litigant. If there had been a member of the Church who entertained exceptional views about the question and was opposed to parochial education except as a supplement to that of the public schools, he might have had no interest or only a tepid one in the outcome of the Oregon case. If a California bank held the view of Mr. Justice Holmes that it liked to pay taxes and believed it was purchasing civilization by doing so, it might not only be without interest in the Union Trust Company case but might even file a brief as *amicus curiae* against it. I hasten to add in this instance no such contingency is apprehended by the state tax authority.

A qualification must be interposed in the former of these two instances. Whatever may be the opinion of any particular Roman Catholic on the value and function of parochial schools, he could not help noting that an unmistakable animus against the organization to which he belonged occasioned the legislation. The State of Oregon at that time had a large number of members belonging to the weird society called the Ku Klux Klan and the legislature was much under their influence. In a definite and real sense, any member of the group of Catholics was adversely affected by the law by the mere fact of his membership. And he was so affected whatever his personal views or his individual conduct. A special element in his personal relations was attacked and, since it was always impossible in fact to separate phases or elements of personality, he was attacked quite as much as if he had been mentioned by name in the statute.

This brings the group into the presence of the law in a thoroughly real and in a somewhat different way from that in which the group of bankers is present before the court in the other case. It is quite true that a statute might well be passed intended to abolish bankers or to render their activities difficult. In the community to which I belong there are many of my fellow citizens who think such a statute would be a great public service. If the tax of which the banks complain had been so motivated, the plaintiff bank in this case would be bringing the whole group of banks into the court with him. The banking function is the one common characteristic of these various groups of persons operating in corporate form, and the judgment, by its direct effect and not merely by furnishing an example, would restrain or relieve all the groups simultaneously in the performance of that function. When a statute or a legal rule, or the absence of one, affects a group in this fashion the operation of the law is different from its operation in regard to individuals.

Whenever groups are involved, the legal process moves appreciably away from its contact with logic. It is well if from time to time reference is made to the reputed rightness of the reasons on which action is taken and logic thus given a certain recognition. The point is, of course, that the characteristically legal machinery, consisting of a court and its variously differentiated lawyers, was never devised for such questions. They are essentially matters of social, political, and economic policy and it is a policy-forming machinery that should handle them.

This is particularly evident in what is the most important of group questions dealt with by courts today, the questions of labor. So far as labor is organized in quasi-corporate form, in trade unions, it can be dealt with as other corporations are dealt with. But so far as labor is an economic grouping, describing those persons who depend for their livelihood on wages earned chiefly by manual effort or dexterity, the interests of such a group can be dealt with in our courts only with extreme difficulty.

It is not merely the fact that the group is so vast in size. That, however, is an important element. When we make our economic division of the community, we list labor as one of a number of the groups that compose our society, and there is always a temptation to suppose that one group out of so many means a fraction of which the total number is the denominator. The larger the number of groups the smaller the fraction. And to that is added the fact that an imaginary residuum, called the public or the state or the community, is set over against all the groups taken together, which thus, even when they are all added up, amount to only one half.

This, being mathematics, is logic, but it is a logic posing as experience and easily unmasked as an impostor as soon as we really examine experience. Labor is a far greater part of our state than any other economic group except that designated as agriculture, and these two together leave so small a number to be distributed among other economic groups that the two might well claim in a democratic state to be the community for many purposes. Certainly they have a good claim for being called "the public" and in most specific civic communities, where conflicts between labor men and employers arise, labor alone is very nearly a major part of "the public."

But not merely because of size and numbers but because of our economic and social history, a labor controversy is not the same thing as a litigation between John Doe and Richard Roe. The commercial revolution of the seventeenth century and the industrial revolution of the nineteenth century created an economic order unique in history. Far from being an ancient order established since the beginning of civilized life, it is a relatively recent one. That there should be so desperate resistance to change of any kind on the part of those who control its operations cannot be based upon a long and immemorial tradition of experience.

But one of the special characteristics of our system is the extreme intricacy of its organization and the delicacy of its mechanism. Change of any kind seems to imperil the whole structure and is resisted without reference to demonstrable danger. However, so far as labor is concerned, only progressive, far-reaching, and relatively rapid changes will produce the sort of adjustment by which laboring men can protect themselves from the extreme consequences of any defects in our economic machinery—and it is nowhere claimed that it is not defective.

One of these extreme consequences is that of being the first victims of the cyclical movements declared to be inherent in the system; or again of being the first victims of cataclysms like war or erosion. In every labor controversy, the issue goes not only beyond the interests of the specific litigants but even beyond the interests of an existing class. It involves a vast economic policy.

On the other side, the group of interests that can be placed in contrast with that of labor is also a complicated and unmanageable one. When the terminology of labor litigation arose, it was possible to speak of labor and capital, employers and employees, and, in any given case, it was possible to see the employers and employees. When photography was invented, one could take pictures of them.

The employers owned and managed their shops, and engaged their workmen. And this remained true when there were many employees and when the operating staff became fairly numerous and differentiated. But under modern conditions, although we can still recognize the employees, can, if we like, assemble them in mass meetings and take flashlight pictures of them, it is not so easy to recognize the employers.

The book of Berle and Means on *The Modern Corporation*[13] has called our attention to this fact and has demonstrated it with a wealth of documentation. Management and what is called ownership are almost wholly separated under modern conditions of industry. The book in question is the kind of book that ought to have been epoch-making so far as our terminology is concerned, but it has not appreciably

13. A. Berle and G. Means, *The Modern Corporation* (1932).

changed either the language of law or of economics so far as this situation is concerned.

It is by no means easy to see whether the employers are those who manage the business, who have also invested some money in it and make direct and sometimes astounding profits out of it; or whether they are the investors scattered over the world who have bought stocks and bonds in it, and who are separated into a number of often conflicting groups; or whether the financial and fiscal agents of these investors, the banks, are the employers—and in these banks we have again the question of management and ownership to consider and an interrelation between the groups of management of the banks and the actual industrial plant to keep in mind. Out of sheer compassion, I say nothing of the additional complication of one industrial plant owned in whole or in part by another or federated or associated with another.

Who are the litigants under these conditions in a labor controversy? Who is the real party in interest[14] in whose name our Codes of Civil Procedure declare all actions must be brought? If any one of the groups contrasted with labor is the "owner" which one, if we give proper consideration of the facts, has most immediate and direct interest in the maintenance of any particular plant? Which one has most interest that there should be a profit from it? And which one most interest that it shall be permanently maintained?

We can get any answer we want by logic, by perfectly sound logic in this case and without imposture.

14. N.Y. Code of Civil Procedure (orig. draft), §91; First Rep. of Code Commissioners, note 2, pp. 123–125; Clark, Chas., "Code Cause of Action," 33 *Yale Law Journal*, 817.

Most of the groups have in some way asserted their claim to some substantial ownership interest in the industrial plant. It is not too clear how any one of these interests is different from that of labor. And an interest in the physical plant has of course been asserted by labor, crudely in the form of the sit-down strike. The problem of recognizing and securing such an interest will doubtless be considered seriously somewhere some time, and it certainly deserves serious consideration.

In that case, we have no employer and employee situation to regulate, but various types of investment—property, direction, labor—whose conflicting claims would not be dealt with in the ordinary fashion, in any case.

To deal adequately with one part of our penal problem—the disposition of the offender—lawyers should be penologists. In such matters as labor questions, the least that can be required of lawyers is that they should be labor-economists. That is well in the way of accomplishment, since a great many lawyers are nothing less than that. Fortunately so sharp a segregation as that which concentrates functions in the penologist is unnecessary here. Lawyers and economists are brothers under their sheepskins.

That the lawyer on the bench should be an economist is a great deal to ask of a busy man who is already required to be a statesman, a logician, a psychologist, a penologist, and a rhetorician—besides being a lawyer. But unless he is an economist, I am afraid there is no answer to the demand that a new type of tribunal be devised in which the judge will

be an economist or flanked by economists. Where that
will fit into the system of tribunals now existing is a
problem of the future.

Is the same thing true for all other types of economic interests that can be considered organized into
groups? It does not quite follow, which you will notice is a logical phrase. In the case of business organi-
zations, the group interest is, we must suppose, rejected out of hand by the groups themselves. Every
now and then, as in the illustration I have offered of
the California banks, there is a specific point in which
a representative may be selected to test what can most
conveniently be tested that way. But ordinarily one
business will not be benefited by what is gained by another. On the contrary, on the theory which businessmen declared to be their most prized possession, it is
as likely as not to be injured by anything which helps
a competitor. Business is assumed to be managed on a
vigorously competitive basis. People who sell goods
do not wish to bargain collectively with those who buy
them. If and when they do, we shall have a reorganized society to deal with in which the need of group
settlements rather than individual ones will become as
imperative as in the case of labor.

There is a special difficulty in the case of agriculture which as an economic interest rivals or exceeds
labor in the number of persons concerned. The group
interest of farmers is often ventilated in legislatures
but rarely in courts. To the extent that farmers are
businessmen, the competitive theory blocks the assertion of group demands. To the extent that farmers
are laborers, there is as yet little sense of collectivity.

Future developments will doubtless put a new color to the entire complex of relationships of the farm population.

The difficulties which the law encounters, when instead of by twos and threes men appear before the court by companies and classes, are definite indications that the courts as at present constituted have only a limited capacity to deal with these large aggregations. Questions of economic policy can be best dealt with by administrative and legislative groups which specifically set out to determine such policy. Only so far as the courts in constitutional questions are active participants in this policy-forming process do these matters come within the scope of the characteristic instrument of the law, the court.

This is tantamount to saying that the most specifically legal of legal agencies, the trial court, is scarcely fitted to deal with matters of large public policy at all. Generally, in constitutional questions, the court of first instance rarely gives more than a tentative judgment. The appellate courts in which these matters are threshed out are in regard to such questions almost conciliar in their nature, and hark back to the time when the King's High Court of Parliament and his Court of the King's Bench were often described by the same name, that of *magna curia*.

It may not be necessary to create new machinery for every new combination and dissolution of entwined human interests which are found to be part of the experience that a court deals with. But there is a constant danger that the fact that the same machinery is used will make it seem the same thing. Courts may take the ambitious stand that nothing human is alien to them but, if they do, they should remember that nothing human is the same on two successive days or in two changed relations.

I should like at this point to permit myself a digression. When we speak of "The Law" or "our law," we are speaking of something limited in space but not in time. But for experience we must take the time factor into consideration. It is the fourth dimension, or the fifth—as you like. We cannot directly experience the law except at the unique moment of time when a law-man pronounces a judgment—or is contemplated as pronouncing a judgment—between two persons.

This moment of time that identifies and determines the event which is the judgment is one of a series of such moments and the term "time" itself is merely a name for this series. It exists by itself as little as length or breadth or thickness does. "Our law" or "The Law" is the series of these legal moments and is, therefore, a matter of history.

I suppose that because I spoke of the dead past, on the basis of which the living present—which, for us, is another name for the imminent future—is to be judged, I have seemed definitely to take my place with those many persons who profess a dislike for history because it is an account of things that are past and dead. I mean here and now to repudiate that association.

When I said it was futile to determine obligations of the present by exclusive reference to the dead past, I mean no disparagement of the past. I have spent a great deal of time with the dead past, indeed with a past that has been dead for several thousand years. I have found it immensely—I use the word in its strict sense—pleasant and profitable. I think there is a great deal to be said for the assertion that many of those who affect to despise history would be somewhat better equipped for all purposes of thinking and acting if they knew a little of it.

The law of any community is history. I do not mean merely that it is determined by history. It is history itself quite as much as the development of the political, the social, or the economic structure of society. Every lawyer is a historian since to cite a case —any case—is to cite a historical document which ought to be dealt with as a problem in historical research.

It is quite true that lawyers are for the most part extremely bad historians. They often make up an imaginary history and use curiously unhistorical methods. And that is true not merely of our rather unlearned bar, but can be illustrated in the far more imposing tribunals of England. I might cite a recent example in the House of Lords, in the case of *Stephens* vs. *Snell* [1939] 3 All E.L.R. 622 (ch.), in which the question arose whether a grant of fisheries by the Crown had been made before or after Magna Carta. That fact would determine the validity of the grant. There is a deal of research entered into as to whether the King Henry mentioned in one of the documents was Henry III or Henry II, and the statement is made that it has been "established" that the right of the Crown to grant fisheries in navigable waters was abolished by Magna Carta. This "establishing," however, turns out to be merely a similar statement in a case in 1862 (*Malcomson* vs. *O'Dea*,

10 H.L.C. 593, 618), which cites other cases. Unfortunately these other cases do not say so at all. And still more unfortunately Magna Carta has not a word to say on the subject. The passage, as historians have long known, as Plowden knew, as Sir Matthew Hale knew, had a different sense. But the statement is found in Blackstone without citation and comes from a casual statement in Coke's *Institutes.* That would be worse than no authority in such matters, because Coke is almost never right on any question of history. But even Coke does not say a word about the restriction of the prerogative in the matter of grants of fisheries, although he manages to misunderstand the passage in Magna Carta in another way, relying on the preposterous Mirrour. The House of Lords case quotes neither Blackstone nor Coke but relies for the determination of a historical fact on another case which simply says there was such a historical fact.

There was the less reason for this pseudohistory, because in several books published between 1862 and 1939, in which real historical methods were applied, the error has been pointed out.[15] This eminent tribunal, however, had apparently neither the courage to say that history was irrelevant, which it might well have said, since the decision of the House of Lords in 1868 was binding by itself, nor the industry to determine what the historical fact was.

This, of course, is only one example of many, though it must be conceded that there are also examples of much better history in both English and

15. McKechnie, W. S., *Magna Carta* (2d ed., 1914), pp. 303–304, esp. 344. Cf. Moore, Stuart A., and Moore, H. S., *History and Law of Fisheries* (1903), p. 13.

American reports. But in most instances, while aware that very old law is history—antiquities they love to call it—the courts are unaware that recent law is equally history and needs quite as much the application of historical methods.

We have thus imposed a new burden on the lawyer on the bench. Besides all the other things asked of him, he is also to be a historian. But there is no help for it. There is simply no way by which the law can be made either simple or easy.

V.

THIS leaves the lawyer somewhat entangled in functions that he can scarcely have consciously undertaken to perform. It seems too bad to add another. But this one, I very much fear, he will have to assume, even if by some miracle he should succeed in shifting the burden of all the others on the shoulders of penologists, economists, politicians, psychologists, and the rest. The lawyer must have something to do with justice.

We began with a statement that law begins in the mind of Zeus. To many men, the important question was less the source of law than its goal. And for that an ancient answer also is at hand. Its goal or its purpose is to achieve justice.

In the second century A.D. an extremely legalistic lawyer, which is to say a mathematically minded one, Publius Juventius Celsus—he had four additional names which I shall spare you—said that law was nothing more or less than the art of achieving justice, *jus est ars boni et aequi*.[1] The term that he used, *bonum et aequum*, is more usually translated as "equity" and it happens to be used by Celsus very nearly in the sense of a body of determinate law, much as "equity" is used by Anglo-American lawyers. Nonetheless, the phrase does not quite mean what our Chancery "equity" meant and for the present may be taken as equivalent to the word "justice" as it is used in ordinary English speech. That law is

1. *Digest,* I, 1, 1, pr.

a means to this end, that its goal is justice, that it seeks to establish justice, is not merely a bare assertion of those men who defend the law and its function. Statutes have made it mandatory on courts to make justice their goal. And it has so impressed itself on the public that it is inscribed on courthouses and halls of legislature.

Rudolf von Ihering, whose notion about the duty of the struggle for law I have had occasion to mention, also had a definite notion about the purpose of law. He did not think of it primarily as a means of effecting justice but, as he says, as a means of securing the conditions of life of the community.

This idea, formulated and elaborated in the admirable first volume of his work on *Purpose in Law*,[2] gives him an obvious claim to be regarded as the father, or at least the grandfather, of most of the theorists about socialized law who wrote in the early twentieth century. The authenticity of this lineage will be disputed by some and it is no part of my task to demonstrate it. But we may take the formula as it stands and ask ourselves whether that is really the purpose of law, in any sense that we can understand and apply.

There is no doubt that an announced purpose to secure the conditions of life in any society looks in the first instance to experience rather than to logic. We could not work out by mathematics what these conditions are. And it must be equally clear that if law is to secure them, it is likely that we shall have to de-

2. Ihering, R. von, *Der Zweck im Recht* (3d ed., 1893-98), Vol. I, was translated as "Law as a Means to an End" (1913) in "Mod. Legal Phil. Series," Vol. V.

pend on experience rather than logic to know how that is to be done, since if the study of human society has taught us anything it is that like causes do not produce like effects even if we postulate a relatively static and uniform society.

But it is a fact of experience that no society is either static or uniform and therefore we could not really entertain Von Ihering's purpose in the law, except to formulate what the changing conditions were which in successive overlapping eras have actually been found to underly social life. This indeed is a logical process, but it is an even more futile and barren process, except as a historical study, than the slightly illicit logic which we saw used to connect two phases of experience in the legal analysis I have tried to set forth. It describes a past result which by definition will not be likely to have any appreciable effect on its successors.

But Von Ihering was not thinking primarily of history. And it becomes apparent in his doctrine, as in that of nearly all sociological or socialized theories of law, that the conditions to be secured are not those of the actual society at any given moment, but of a social ideal, which the actual society scarcely even approximates. I do not believe that Von Ihering thought that the bustling and junkerized Prussia in which he lived had approximated very closely to the ideal whose conditions he hoped to secure by law. And it certainly is the fact that most sociological doctrines of law make no such assumption for the society in which their expounders lived.

If we are dealing with an ideal, we have a goal that is given not by logic nor yet by experience, but by a moral conviction. To secure this ideal goal we cannot help having recourse to rational processes. We are hoping for a real if ultimate experience, and we can equally hope that the rational processes that in our calculations ought to lead to it will themselves be realized in experience.

Nonetheless an ideal experience, no matter how earnestly hoped for, is not quite the same thing as experience in the real sense. It is something that can be kept in continuous and permanent relation to both our coördinates, and any theory of law will be as valid as any other under these conditions, provided as in the case of Von Ihering's theory it is honestly derived from the facts of social living and is infused by a moral purpose that can justify itself by accepted standards.[3]

So analyzed, the formula of Von Ihering is not essentially different from that of Publius Juventius Celsus, who was a less humane man and a less philosophic spirit than Von Ihering, even if Josef Kohler refused to concede to Von Ihering elementary philosophic competence.[4] Whatever else justice may turn out to be, it is at least a social ideal, that is to say, an imagined system of living together in a relationship that satisfies some moral standard of right living; and the law that secures this secures the conditions of life in a good society. It is quite true that the justice which Celsus used, and which many generations of lawyers and jurists after him have acclaimed, pro-

3. Jerome Frank, *Law and the Modern Mind* (1930), pp. 217–222.

4. Kohler, Josef, *Philosophy of Law* (Eng. tr. by A. Albrecht, "Mod. Legal Phil. Series," 1921), pp. 11, 25–26.

fessed to be derived from no examination of experience, but solely from contemplation. As a matter of fact, however, it had its source in an irrational—or, if we like, superrational—contact with experience in spite of the pride it took in denying this fact. The sociologists, of course, glory in it.

What is important to note is that either formula, the formula that makes justice the purpose of law and the formula that makes its purpose the securing of the conditions of social life, assigns to the law a field of operation far beyond that which can be verified from experience.

To secure a good society, whether it is good because it is characterized by an abstractly derived justice or by an ideal taken from experience, cannot be the purpose of law for the simple reason that it is the purpose of the entire mechanism of political and social organization. Those who manage our organization must be attempting to secure good conditions of social living. They will not be heard to have anything less in mind.

But the mechanism of law is merely a small part of the mechanism of social management, closely connected with the mechanism of political administration. It is a mechanism difficult to characterize and impossible to relate exhaustively to other parts of the social complex. That is, however, more or less a matter of historical accident. The one thing we can say about the legal mechanism, the court and its complex of institutions, is its limitations, for all the great demands made upon the lawyer. Law can deal with large social policies and purposes only indirectly and to a small degree, with the one exception of constitutional law within which field in the United States it wields a power more than coördinate with the power of other governmental institutions.

To assign to this legal mechanism the task of securing a proper social system of living is to place upon it a burden far beyond its capacities. We must recall that even within the class of relationships that the law regards as its special province, those arising out of commercial transactions, nearly all the large arrangements are made by business custom or by specific regulations of trades themselves. The law in its proper sense, the law of the trial court in which a judge delivers a judgment of "may" or "ought," is concerned chiefly with marginal and exceptional situations, with determining whether a given situation is within the scheme which custom or group legislation has created, or whether it has been omitted. Or else the purpose of law in dealing with a great many forms of economic disturbance is conciliation and appeasement, sometimes avowed and sometimes concealed.

Not justice or a good society, therefore, but convenience of commercial practice, appeasement of individual quarrels, or an increase of good will among competitors, if that is possible, is the purpose of law if we examine its actual operation. And to these three purposes other purposes can be added, such as the direction of the domestic policies of the country in constitutional questions or the elimination of nonoffenders from the group of punishable persons. The purposes are not coördinate, are not the same in quality, do not operate within the same social sphere, and are called by the common name of legal only because the same institution, the court, performs some function in the realization of all of them. Where does justice enter?

We have been speaking of justice, the *bonum et aequum* of Celsus, as though we knew exactly what it was. And, of course, every child knows what justice is. This sentence is to be taken quite literally. The persons who explain with a knowing wink that law has, of course, nothing to do with justice have usually exactly the notion of justice that a child has, which is that it is something of which the child approves largely because it is to its advantage.

The grown-up notion of justice, whether entertained by lawyers or laymen, by ethical philosophers or practical citizens, so long as it is an honest notion, is, of course, a very different thing. But that does not mean that it is a clear concept or is easily defined. Definitions of justice have been offered in all civilized communities for at least thirty centuries, but the term has eluded definition so well that two opposing senses have been fused into it. It sometimes suggests harshness and sometimes mercy and charity. As far as the word "justice" itself is concerned, it seems to begin with a calculus of equality, recompense exactly balancing conduct, merit obtaining its deserved reward, crime its inexorably due punishment. On this last side, it involves a notion of retaliation which is derived from the term "talion," and which still dominates both our practice and our suppressed theory in the treatment of offenders. On the civil side it is the origin of consensual obligation in what was called the *jus gentium*. There justice is an idea which in philosophic speculation is honored with the term of "commutative justice," and in the later common law it became the more prosaic *quid pro quo*.

This sort of calculus of compensation is supremely logical, and in it the original accounting sense of *logos* is unmistakably apparent. For the purpose of determining this kind of justice we seem to need nothing except mathematics, a delicate balance, as the words recompense and compensation might have warned us. The one great difficulty is that this calculation can never be mathematically accurate, since the equality is at best an approximation. The only mathematical equality is identity.

All that commutative justice could give us is therefore a rather arbitrary equalization by means of an appraisal that will rarely completely satisfy both parties.[5] This type of equalization was rendered appreciably easier for commercial matters by the invention of money. But even here complete satisfaction can scarcely be guaranteed as some of the appraisals in corporate management and reorganization may teach us, not to speak of the process of valuation for purposes of taxation. The common law which declared that any *quid* equaled any *quo* was easier to handle than the late Roman law doctrine of lesion which drew the line at a *quid* that was less than half its compensatory *quo*.

If our approximation gets to be fairly close, and for a great many business matters in a money economy it can be made to be fairly close, justice of this

5. We may compare the definition of equity, which is the medieval equivalent of justice, given by Bracton, IV, 186a. *Aequitas est convenientia rerum quae cuncta coaequiparat.* This is cited by Coke, 1 *Inst.* §21, with complete approval.

first stage is measurably achieved. Retaliatory justice in crime was achieved with some degree of precision in primitive society but only in the case of may-
hem, or in some types of homicide. In other penal
matters, compensation early gave way to reasons of
state in the form of a rapid increase in capital punishment—a phenomenon that repeats itself over and
over again whenever persons of primitive minds get
into control of communities, as in the case of Nazi
Germany.

The lady called Justice who sits or stands in marble on the pediments of our public buildings, holding
the scales to weigh the *quid* against the *quo*, and the
sword to take the head for head, limb for limb, is of
course justice in this first stage and the bandage
about her eyes indicates that in her opinion mathematics, the inevitableness of the equalization, will relieve her from the burden of making any estimate of
her own.

She is a formidable and stern person, this Justice
of scales and sword, and it is hard to realize that she
was at one time ardently desired. It is, however, a fact
that justice, even this coldly calculating, inexorable
and mathematical justice, seemed in the early stages
of civilized society to guarantee peace and stability.
As against the domination of the stronger and the
craftier, even the harshest rule of talion, the crudest
tariff of compensations, was a refuge and a hope.

We cannot tell just when human experience dis-
covered that this calculating justice would not do and
when the esthetic thrill of a precise equation, assuming we have agreed to call it precise, came somehow

into conflict with a consideration different in kind and quality.

This new consideration was based on a sense of human feeling as well as a need for human society. The computation by equivalents in penal law produced a real danger of reducing effective soldiers. More than that, however, the allowances which men in close association almost instinctively make for each other meant that the judge-magistrate—also a member of the community—could scarcely help taking into account the need for such allowance.

Notions like indulgence, kindness, mercy, forgiveness are earlier and better established than a wholly cynical view of man as an essential brute will have us believe. Notions like conciliation and compromise are almost as old as feud and warfare. Indeed, they may be quite as old because they may be corollaries of it. And in all of them, the mathematics of computation and compensation is inevitably sacrificed. There can be little doubt, too, that consciously or subconsciously the inaccuracy of that computation left men uneasy as to the validity of their justice.

Out of a sense that men must not always be held fully answerable for all their acts, combined with a realization that to hold them answerable was likely to demand too much or too little of them, and further out of what—at the risk of being denominated a sentimentalist—I dare to call the human instinct of compassion or mercy, a different standard of judgment was created. It was given many names. We know it as equity, as the Romans did, since they often equated *aequitas* with *clementia* or *humanitas*. The Greek *epieikeia* came to have a meaning like this. But what-

ever the word was that was used, we find almost as
early as we find a magistrate-judge, two sorts of justice, a hard and a soft, a stricter and a looser, a
lower and a higher, or, if we like, simple justice and
a more complex sort.[6]

One of our difficulties is the matter of terminology,
as in so many other human affairs. Those two types
or degrees or kinds of justice have interchanged
terms from time to time and have been complicated
with politics, economics, and sociology. In the two organized legal systems whose history we know best,
that of Rome and England, it was further complicated by the fact that the stricter justice was a privilege out of which demands arose which had no relation even to equivalence between what was asked and
what was rendered. And both these historical systems
during the Middle Ages had perforce to live in some
relation with a wholly different system in which the
kind of justice administered was theoretically always
the higher, looser, softer, and more complex sort.
"Justice" came to have a rather sinister sense in the
Middle Ages, when "high justice" was as high as the
lord's private gallows and "low justice" as low as a
noisome hole under the floor of his castle, and when
the word "justice" itself might mean a gibbet or an
executioner.

A further complication was introduced by the
terms "natural" and "reasonable"—both of which
seem to come into our law from Chrysippus and his
cohorts. If the strict law was a privilege, it could be
challenged not only on the ground that it was strict

6. Cf. "A Juster Justice, A More Lawful Law," *Essays in Tribute to O. K. McMurray* (1935), pp. 537–564.

and harsh but also that it was "unnatural" and "unreasonable." But when a reasonable basis was insisted upon, the avowed premise was usually a sense of humanity which is hardly a matter of reason or computation.

It was too much to expect that these terms would always be kept straight or that all the vague and variously shaded and colored notions in them would always be sharply differentiated. And, as a matter of fact, popular feeling has wavered as much as ethical philosophers and legal theorists—although it cannot be said that it has wavered more. When there is a popular clamor for "justice," it regularly indicates that a violent thirst for vengeance has been aroused which will normally be satiated only by the ancient law of talion. But "justice" is also invoked when a harsh decision is rendered or a claim enforced against persons who are deemed to deserve special consideration.

The "justice" by which I have translated Celsus' *bonum et aequum* is, as I have said, more precisely equity. Equity, as Celsus imagined it, was not the Aristotelian equity which merely made exceptions possible in a slightly overdefinite general rule, nor yet the other concept of equity which meant being willing, out of human charity, to take less than one had a legal right to ask. It was the equity which attempted to substitute a general rule suitable to all civilized .communities for a historical rule which had grown up more or less at haphazard in a special one. What the formula of Celsus implies is that law is the inchoate state and justice the perfected form.

Unfortunately it also suggests the doctrine that if

lawyers will tend to their business, which is legal technique—that is to say, the application of formulas or rules derived from statutes and precedents—the final result will be justice, if the rules are good rules and the technique precise. A good rule is a carefully formulated one and a precise technique is one that can almost be mechanically applied.

It is safe to say that Celsus himself thought that this was so, since he was very much of a precisian. He would have gone beyond the rules of older Roman law and derived his premises from a larger system which covered most men, provided these men were very much like the Greeks and Romans Celsus knew. This was something of a concession to humanity, but even when so enlarged, the end of law was a thing that was achieved only by the law.

The psychological attitude of the lawyer to whom justice is the end of law is one that renders the achievement of the end a little doubtful. The end after all of most activities can easily be pushed far away. And when the activity is so complicated and the technique so hard as that of the law, it is fatally easy to get absorbed in it and proceed in the comfortable assurance that justice can hardly help from emerging at the other end of the machine, if it is well constructed and well managed.

More important than all these considerations is the fact that justice is far too large a matter to be merely the perfect result of the perfect technique of law. I hope we shall have a chance to glance briefly at some of the obvious aspects of the concept of justice, but no glance can really be so cursory as to suppose that the machinery of courts—taken in its largest and most comprehensive sense—is enough to secure this fundamentally important element in civilized institutions.

How does justice enter into the legal process at all? The earliest differentiation of the Norman King's Council established a body like the Exchequer which was required to pass on disputes between royal officials and royal subjects, and was thus brought face to face with the problem of a standard. The problem was briefly solved. They were to judge *secundum aequitatem*[7]—"according to equity," which was merely a general term for justice. Of course, they knew what equity was. Who could be ignorant of that? But in the course of the development of the common law, to judge *secundum aequitatem* was pushed into the position of a supplement. There were gaps in the law, *casus omissi*, cases of new impression, and to fill these rare and slightly discreditable gaps, equity—justice—humanity—would do very well.

Equity or justice, however, entered the legal process surreptitiously in another way. The legal technique that had justice as a remotely envisaged goal but could dispense with it as a daily guide and monitor was a technique of logical inference from statutes and precedent. It was fondly believed—and, despite Holmes and Cardozo, it is still believed—that a fixed gaze at statute and precedent will automatically yield a formula, which can be called a rule or if it is broad enough even a principle, and that by letting

7. Glanville, *De Legibus et Cons. Regni Angliae*, II, 12; VII, 1 (Woodbine's ed. with note at p. 225).

loose the forces of logic upon this detached formula a conclusion can be reached which will move irresistibly to a final just goal. Unfortunately the statute or precedent is almost necessarily equivocal. A number of formulas detach themselves from them and a selection must be made.

What is the basis of the selection? It might be a purely arbitrary preference for one formula as a premise that will lead to an arbitrarily desired conclusion. Nor can there be any doubt that the conclusion often becomes desirable for reasons that will not bear a severe test of impartiality or scientific objectiveness. Evidently prepossessions must count here and economic and social prepossessions are common and deep rooted.

But it is clearly and demonstrably not the case that these prepossessions are always and constantly in the mind of the judge in determining judgments. And when they are unconscious they fuse into the stuff of which his mind is composed as a whole. In the majority of cases it is certainly hard to see any relation between even the unconscious economic and social biases of the court and the result of its decisions. One of my distinguished predecessors in this series, Dean Pound, has examined the fate of *Rylands* vs. *Fletcher* in various American states and found no relation between the determinations and the economic backgrounds of the state as a whole.[8] If it were proved that the judges in these states were selected from a class that did not share what might be conjectured to

8. Pound, Roscoe, *Introduction to the Philosophy of Law* (1922), pp. 183–186.

be the economic views of the state as a whole, a relation might nonetheless be established, but it is unlikely that such proof can be furnished.

In the great majority of cases, a court which must select a formula from equivocal generalizations presented by statute or precedent will be guided by a vague sense of right and would assert that it was guided by justice. And this sense of justice is part of the court's moral and mental equipment.

How is this sense of justice to be distinguished from an inveterate personal prejudice? How is it to be distinguished from a whimsical oddity of feeling? The answer can be based only on the extent to which it is shared by other persons.[9]

Justice is an idea. Because it is an idea which infuses a sort of glow, it is also an emotion. But an idea, it is vital to remember, has no objective existence. An idea is someone's idea—in this case the idea of a judge, a decidedly flesh-and-blood gentleman and consequently unique. His idea or ideas are also unique. How can that be justice which is different from man to man? And how can the sneers of practical lawyers at "fireside justice" and "cadi-justice"— which assume whimsicality and arbitrariness on the part of the judge—how can these sneers be met or refuted? It is to prevent whimsicality and arbitrariness that the judge has been more and more restricted by statute, that the theory of precedent was created, and that in systems that profess to reject precedent, scholastic and academic authoritative tra-

9. Cf. "The Chancellor's Foot," 49 *Harvard Law Review*, 44, 49–50.

dition has been put in its place. Has there really been
no progress in the law in all these millennia?

I am not certain whether it is of the highest importance to decide that progress is desirable; but it
can easily be shown, I think, that the fear that the
conscious recognition of a sense of justice will result
in whimsicality is insubstantial. For while in one sense
an idea is in one man's mind and nowhere else, it is a
fact that within any given community and with the
specific unity of man to begin with, individuals, however unique, have a number of points in common.
Such common denominators are demonstrable. The
notion in the heads of any two persons about justice
are likely to be different. If the number is multiplied,
the points of difference will be increased. But even if
we multiply the number by thousands we shall not
eliminate the common denominators present in all
these notions.

These common denominators of the various individual notions of justice—a hodgepodge of unrelated
factors, it may be—constitute the idea of justice that
can get itself objectified by being written with a capital letter. Any imaginative person who so desires may
dress justice up and carve her in marble or cast her
in bronze, or paint her—with or without sword and
scales—in the mural decorations of courts and legislative chambers. She will be of somewhat miscellane-
ous and heterogeneous origin, no matter how she is
dressed and equipped.

This justice, composed of what we can find in common in the notions of justice that are entertained by
a large number of men, would be a rather bare out-

line, if we attempted to include all men in a given community, and would still be little more than a skeleton, if we took it from a group chosen purely by the sampling process. But if the persons from whom we take it are those who to begin with have certain common stuff in their minds, we shall doubtless have a much larger aggregation of elements and they will be elements easier to fit into a common system.

In the last analysis, justice must be the common denominator of what a specific group—the judges themselves—think is just. It is not a mere mechanical summing up. The thoughts in this subject of the Supreme Court of the United States—or rather of a majority of them—are vastly important for a great many purposes and fairly irrelevant for other purposes. The thoughts of distinguished judges in busy jurisdictions will contribute more elements to our construction than those of other judges in jurisdictions less likely to have wide experience in different fields.

But however weighted there will be a considerable number of common elements, for there is a great deal that is common in the education and environment of all our judges. If we had a situation like that of England of the early nineteenth century, we could assume without much likelihood of error that the sense of justice in the mind of a judge would make him feel that the stopping of fox-earths was worse than the destruction of a farmer's crops, and that it was just that a small group of propertied men should be permitted to arrange their marital difficulties by divorce but that men without property should not. We should know that, because the majority of judges came of families in which a great deal of value in society was attributed to the sport of fox hunting and to the possession of property.

Our American judges are less accountable because the range of education and origin is much wider, but there is still a substantial list of things that we might assume they regarded as fundamentally just and a decision which contradicted any of them would so disturb a judge that if he were not in some way coerced into rendering it, he would not do so.[10]

Evidently the elements in the judge's mind which create—or which are—his sense of justice can prove their right to be called so, if enough of them are common to a large and variously derived group of persons—chiefly judges. There is clearly no sense of whimsicality nor any reason for assuming arbitrariness in an idea which is common to a large number of persons performing a common function.

There is a curious tendency in lawyers, when they speak of justice, and in ethical philosophers as well, to run into metaphors. Justice has been called— among many other things—the steering wheel of law or the port to which the law sails. Josef Kohler rejected both these metaphors and asserted that Justice was the star by which the helmsman steered.[11] As poetry, one will do as well as another. I remember a book written by a famous constitutional lawyer in which the Constitution was successively—almost si-

10. Cf. "A Theory of Judicial Decisions or How Judges Think," 11 *American Bar Association Journal* (1925), pp. 357–359.

11. Kohler, Josef, *Moderne Rechtsprobleme*, p. 18.

multaneously—a rock, a lighthouse, a raft, and—unless my memory plays me a trick—a haven.[12] Justice may be all these things, but the justice that will serve our purposes must also be a process of moral valuation tinged with a kind of humane emotion.

When the Preacher who was King in Jerusalem ended his beautiful and despondent summary of the futility of life and effort, he found that the conclusion of the whole matter was to fear God and keep His commandments. The commandments he had in mind were many and quite specific, and their observance would occupy a man sufficiently to make consideration of justice and injustice external and somewhat irrelevant.

A wholly different person, the Syro-Phoenician Greco-Roman, Domitius Ulpianus, attempted to find the conclusion of the whole matter, so far as the law was concerned, in only three commandments (*praecepta*), often enough quoted, *honeste vivere, neminem laedere, suum cuique tribuere*.[18] These have at times been sharply derided as three repetitions of an injunction to act justly. They may, however, be understood as slightly less vague counsels of perfection. Paraphrased, they amount to a demand on us to respect the person and property of others and to conduct oneself with a sense of personal dignity—for that is implicit in *honeste*.

Ulpian called them commandments that summed up the law, which, following Celsus, he took to be a

12. Beck, James, *The Constitution of the United States* (1925), reviewed by Thomas Reed Powell in 41 *New Republic*, 314–315.
18. *Digest*, 1, 1, 10, pr. *Inst. Just.*, I, 1, 3. These are probably the most famous phrases of the Roman law. Cf. Blackstone, *Comm.*, I.

means of securing equity or justice. But the objection often raised to them is that they beg the question so far as justice is concerned, and this objection is, I think, quite unanswerable. Personal integrity, property, and social dignity are valuable things, but to recognize them is difficult for the mind unillumined by a sense of justice.

And this sense of justice unfortunately is to be found in neither of our coördinates of logic and experience. If it were the strict or the simple justice of talion and compensation, it lends itself somewhat to calculation and may be made a matter of mathematics and logic. Again, if we look wholly to experience, we can scarcely get further than customary action out of which we can at best derive the satisfaction that our conduct is not aberrant, that we are as other men. But justice or equity or *epieikeia* is not satisfied by logic or even by conformity. It introduces as a standard of valuation a sense of human values in which a strong and passionate feeling for the irreducible dignity of human life itself is the basic measure.

I mean this as no mere flight of rhetoric or vague metaphor. Immanuel Kant who spent his life in a curiously inhuman isolation and who on any specific practical question would almost certainly have rendered a fantastically unworkable decision, found a formula that men living in warmer contact with their fellows can use. "No man," he declared, "may be considered merely as a means to an end of another man."[14]

Aristotle's equity or *epieikeia* was a mere correc-

14. Kant, Immanuel, *Grundlegung zur Metaphysik der Sitten*, II, 54, ed. by Buchenau and Cassirer 1913, IV, pp. 286–287.

tion of the overstatement or understatement inherent in all general classifications. It was something better than justice but better for what might be called logical reasons.[15] The Platonic justice was an exact equivalent between function and capacity.[16] It included equity or *epieikeia* which was merely a type of enlightenment that made it possible to arrive at justice. It was this idea that got itself rather woodenly formulated by the Stoics and reappears in the famous formula of Celsus.

But there was a parallel and humanly more satisfactory—emotionally satisfactory—doctrine which declared that the better kind of justice was determined by an irrational sense of human brotherhood, by a concession to humanity which in this case was the same as humaneness. It is specifically called a lessening of demands, an *elattosis*.[17] In later Roman law and in medieval law whenever the notion of a better justice than the harsh and compensatory *justitia* appears, it is often roundly called clemency and mercy. It was the justice that just men who are also humane men will apply when they are judges.[18]

Just men are men who are so far Kantians that

15. Aristotle, *Nichomachean Ethics*, 1137a–1138b, V, 10–11. "The equitable is just, but not the legally just but a correction of legal justice. . . . The equitable is just and better than one kind of justice—[it is] a correction of the law where it is defective because of universality" (translated by W. D. Ross).

16. The subtitle of Plato's most famous book, *The Republic*, is "On Justice." The entire book is a development of the thesis that "justice" demands a perfect harmony both in the individual and in the state in which he lives.

17. Pseudo-Plato, *Definitiones*, 412b.

18. Cf. "A Juster Justice, A More Lawful Law," *Essays in Tribute to O. K. McMurray* (1935), pp. 561–563; *Early Greek Concepts of Equity*, Mnemosyna Pappoulias (1934), pp. 217–218.

they do not think of other men as a means to their ends, not even when the others are concededly and immeasurably inferior to themselves. Cruelty and exploitation are the fundamental evils of society. Just men are those who will not gratify their brute sense of superiority through the sufferings of other men or use other men solely in order to increase their own advantage. To eliminate cruelty and exploitation is possible only by increasing the number of just men.

It is idle to think of the law *as a means* to this end. It can be attained only with advancing civilization and if one thing is clear it is that civilization advances not in a steady forward movement but by fits and starts, with recessions and recoils. We may well be in a period of recession now, as Western Europe was at the beginning of the seventh century. So far as those are concerned who think of law in its relation to other social forces, the only active participation they can have in the process of advancing civilization is to insist consciously on the opportunities that just men may find in the technique of legal judgment and neither to belittle the opportunity nor to impose upon it a moral obligation that will render it futile.

The law is not right reason, nor the means of a good life, nor the framework of society, nor the foundation of the world, nor the harmony of the spheres. It is a technique of administering a complicated social mechanism, so complicated that it reaches at some point almost any sphere of human conduct, but often only barely reaches it. The technique can dispense with neither logic nor experience. But law will not be good law by becoming a consummately perfect technique in regard either to logic or experience. That can be achieved only when just men perform the technical task of the law with the ancient formula before them—*ut inter bonos bene agier oportet*—"as humane men should act when they act humanely."

Humanity is, after all, the business of the law. When the law forgets that, it were well that its right hand should forget its cunning and its eloquent tongue cleave to the roof of its mouth. It will remain in permanent exile by the rivers of Babylon.

INDEX

as cases, 43
as history, 137–140
as prediction of a judgment, 37–39
diversity of purposes in, 146–147
no single method in, 100–101, 125
purposes of, 140–146
research in, 50–52
scholastic in character, 44–45
Lawyers:
  lawyer as advocate, 117
  lawyer as economist, 135
  lawyer as historian, 139–140
  lawyer as penologist, 103, 121
  origin of profession, 41–43
Leibnitz, G. von:
  notation in calculus, 4
Liberty:
  as the goal of law, 108
Liszt, Franz von:
  opposition to fixed penalties, 110
Littleton on Tenures:
  typical book of property law, 124
Logic:
  in constructing experience, 45
  in procedure and evidence, 58
  in proof, 56
  indispensable in speech, 98
  syllogisms in, 1, 11, 112–113
  used in legal technique, 154
Logos:
  orthos logos, 3, 8
Luke, Gospel of:
  Apocryphal passage in, 98

Magna Carta:
  historically misconstrued in fisheries case, 138–139
Maitland, F. W.:
  on regal style of Elizabeth, 31
Malcomson vs. *O'Dea,* 138

Margin:
  in social experience, 28, 29
Marshall, John:
  on hearsay evidence, 61
Mathematics:
  static in character, 6–7, 60, 113
The Max Morris vs. *Curry,* 73 n. 2
Mina Queen vs. *Hepburn,* 61 n. 11
Mirrour of Justices:
  unreliable as source of history, 139
Montesquieu, Charles de:
  against "reason of state," 110
Morley, John:
  on compromise, 79
Municipal law:
  meaning of, 5

Negligence:
  in admiralty, 72–73
  suits for, 68–71
Nietzsche, Friedrich:
  inhumanity of doctrine, 93
Notation:
  in law, 3, 9 n. 9
  in mathematics, 4, 5
Nulla poena sine lege:
  fundamental in American criminal law, 110
  study of maxim by J. Hall, 110 n. 4

Ownership:
  complicated title in corporate property, 133

Paine, Thomas:
  defended by Erskine, 118
Party in interest:
  code requisite as plaintiff, 133

www.ingramcontent.com/pod-product-compliance
Lightning Source LLC
Chambersburg PA
CBHW021402090426
42742CB00009B/971